HANG GLIDING
AND
FLYING SKILLS
by DENNIS PAGEN

ILLUSTRATIONS BY THE AUTHOR

to Tom and John and Don
in memory of our fledgling days

CONTENTS

FORWARD. vii
CHAPTER I – HANG GLIDING – AN OVERVIEW 1
   The Past 1
   The Present. 3
   The Gliders 5
   Construction Materials 7
   Hang Gliding and You. 8

CHAPTER II – WHY IT FLIES 10
   The Airfoil 10
   The Flying Wing 13
   Glider Control and Stalls. 14
   Stability 17
   Hang Glider Performance 18
   Summary 23

CHAPTER III – SELECTING YOUR EQUIPMENT. 24
   The Glider. 24
   Building Your Own. 28
   The Harness. 29
   The Helment 33
   Miscellaneous Equipment 33
   Caring For Your Equipment 34
   Summary. 35

CHAPTER IV – BEGINNING FLIGHT 37
   Site Selection 37
   Watching The Wind. 38
   Setting Up. 39
   Ground Handling. 41
   Taking Off. 45
   Level Flight. 47
   Landing. 48
   The End Of The Day. 49
   Summary. 50

CHAPTER V – INTERMEDIATE FLIGHT .51
   Flying In Wind 51
   Turns. 53
   Flying Higher 56
   Landings 57
   Summary. 59

CHAPTER VI – ADVANCED AERODYNAMICS
              AND GLIDER DESIGN........................60
    Structural Strength 60
    Turns..62
    Stalls..67
    Washout And Planform 69
    Performance At Slow Speeds........................71
    Performance At High Speeds........................74
    Summary...76

CHAPTER VII – ADVANCED FLIGHT 77
    Advanced Take-offs....................................77
    The 360...79
    Experiencing Lift 81
    Ridge Soaring 81
    Thermal Soaring 83
    Wave Soaring..87
    Summary...88

CHAPTER VIII – UPGRADING YOUR EQUIPMENT 89
    The High Performer....................................89
    The Harness..90
    Repairing Equipment 91
    Trimming The Glider..................................92
    Summary...94

CHAPTER IX – MORE CHALLENGES.......................95
    Expert Maneuvers 95
    Competition 96
    Cross-Country...97
    Tandem Flying 97
    Fixed Wings..99
    Towing 100
    Engines 102
    Balloon Drops...103
    The Future 104

APPENDIX I...105
APPENDIX II 107
GLOSSARY 108

FORWARD

Have you ever walked through green, rolling hills on a windy spring day? The whole world seems alive as you climb a steep grade, panting for breath. You finally reach the top and lean into the brisk damp air blowing from the south. The view is enchanting. Farmhouses, forests and fields spread out below. Suddenly, you're caught by a childhood memory and you spread your arms. In an instant you're soaring through the air on restless wings, floating with the hawk high overhead; you swoop and whirl with the wind whispering in your ears. All too soon your flight of fantasy is ended and you once again stand on that grassy hilltop. Did you regret the return to reality? There is no cause for regret, for now you can experience the dream of flying free. Simply acquire the skills of man's newest outdoor sport — hang gliding.

This book is all about hang gliding and how you can learn to fly in the easiest and safest manner possible. Hang gliding is fun. From the moment you lift your first set of wings to the time you're inscribing scrolls upon the sky, you will be caught up with the challenge and the pleasure of the sport.

To advance to the expert level of hang gliding, you need to master two things: flying skill and knowledge of flying conditions. Hang Gliding and Flying Skills cover the first topic in great detail and relates to the second topic in a practical manner. This allows a pilot to advance safely and knowledgeably to an intermediate level without having to concentrate on anything but flying practice. The book entitled Hang Gliding and Flying Conditions by the author is a complete source of information concerning all the wind and weather factors a pilot will encounter. The combination of these two books represents the major part of the information available on hang gliding today.

Flying skill consists of two parts itself. These are technique and judgement. The actual control of a hang glider is easy to learn. Judgement comes from a gradual process of practice and evaluation in many different situations. The air is a changing, living entity. This is what provides interest and a variety of situations requiring judgement.

You can learn to fly to an advanced level with just the teachings of this book, insight and a mature attitude. However, there is no substitute for a trained certified instructor. Rather, it is my wish that you will use this material to supplement the learning you receive from the instructor. Most people can't afford to take lessons to the advanced level. This book will provide the guidance needed.

To lend continuity to a pilot's learning process, I have followed the United States Hang Gliding Association Hang Rating Program in the text. The presentation of concepts follows the well planned progression of acquired skills from Hang I to Hang IV. You will find plenty of material to digest between the chapters on instruction. This material was chosen to answer the questions asked most often by students and provide a broad knowledge of the sport.

The essence of hang gliding is enjoyment. I sincerely hope that this book adds to your enjoyment of "surfing the sky". Ease yourself back to an earlier time when you dreamed of a magic carpet adventure. Learn to soar on effortless silent wings.

CHAPTER I

HANG GLIDING – AN OVERVIEW

THE PAST

Man is a restless romantic. He has scaled the awesome mountain craigs, probed the silent ocean depths and now he navigates the skies. It wasn't always so. At one time mankind could only dream of such adventures. Rumors, myths and fables from the dim past indicate that flying was perhaps the most yearned for experience. The graceful flight of the birds inspired legends of the Egyptian Phoenix and Persian Hoama as well as the American Quetzel and Thunderbird. Later, tales like the ever-popular story of Icarus and Daedelus and reports of man carrying kites from Tibet and Japan suggest that some intrepid souls did indeed get airborne. The measure of their success is questionable.

The first historical personage to examine the posibilities of human flight in a totally scientific manner was that matchless genius, Da Vinci. Leonardo spent many hours studying bird flight and wing structure as well as the flow of fluids. From this basic research he designed and began to build a flying craft that in retrospect looks very promising (see figure 1).

FIGURE I. – LEONARDO'S ASSISTANT

An impetuous assistant borrowed the unfinished wings without the master's approval and proceeded to leap from a convenient tower. He eliminated himself from the human race and the grieving Leonardo returned to the invention of more realistic earth-bound machines. The pursuit of flight subsided for several hundred years.

The next important contributor to the cause was the landed gentleman, Sir George Cayley. This brilliant designer built several flying models which he launched from the hills of his English estate. In 1852 he succeeded in towing his coachman aloft in a large glider complete with landing gear. Unfortunately, he was too far ahead of his time.

The fifty years that followed brought about technological advancement to the point that machines took care of much of the labor and thus provided mankind with increased leisure time. An inventor no longer had to be a wealthy aristocrat in order to have time to develop an idea. In addition, there arose a growing demand for entertainment of all sorts. Flying was a good candidate.

A host of brilliant men capitalized on the unlimited design possibilities provided by the growing variety of manufactured materials and the appearance of the gasoline engine. Successful flight was finally achieved around the turn of the century by such men as Montgomery, Pilcher, Chanute and Lillienthal. This was true hang gliding in the sense that their craft were foot launchable and powered by gravity only. Well documented reports from the period indicate that these early experimenters enthusiastically aided new talent with religious zeal. The Wright brothers were two gifted inventors who utilized the existing designs and carried them one step further. With the addition of an engine to their glider, they heralded the birth of modern aviation. Hang gliding took a back seat. The race was on to fly further, higher and faster. A new sport emerged. Men were no longer content with simply gliding down a slope, but insisted on roaring through the sky in heroic fashion.

Things calmed a bit with the unpleasant reality of World War I and economic depression. What emerged was an aviation industry based on military and transportation interests. Eventually, some of the original beauty of flight was recaptured by the development of sailplanes and soaring techniques. However, this sport remained out of reach of the general public due mainly to the high costs involved. The world was still waiting for simple and affordable flying.

The breakthrough first appeared in the late 40's with the invention of the Rogallo wing. The designer, Francis Rogallo, experimented with many configurations, but the most common format consisted of three equal length tubes supporting a flexible triangular sail as in figure 2. Dr. Rogallo was working for the American space program and originally devised the flexible wing as a maneuverable re-entry parachute for manned spacecraft. The success of water retrieval methods, however, eliminated the need for maneuverability and NASA forgot the Rogallo wing.

The design wasn't lost. Many would-be birdmen were intrigued by the suitability for controlled flight and the simplicity of construction. What ensued was a flurry of trial and error experimentation until advancements in the late 1960's resulted in the realization of man's ancient dream – free flight.

Indeed, man could have flown thousands of years ago, using the same Rogallo design and natural materials such as bamboo and silk. However, the popularization of the sport was not feasible until recreation became a major pursuit, roads and automobiles were available to provide ready access to flying sites, construction materials were mass produced and aerodynamic principles understood. It was with the fusion of all these social, economic and technological factors that the present era of hang gliding began.

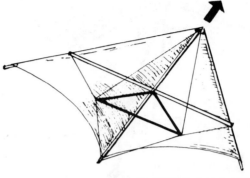

FIGURE 2. — THE ROGALLO WING

THE PRESENT

In 1963, three Australian waterskiers, John Dickenson, Bill Moyes and Bill Bennett traded their flat kites for Rogallo wings. The flat kites were capable of carrying a man skyward when towed behind a boat, but provided little control and could not be released from the tow line. As soon as the Rogallo wing was tried the great potentials were realized. Here was a kite that could be turned, dived and, in time, released to float freely earthward. The first wings were small and unrefined but the neophyte pilots quickly enhanced their skills, flying higher and longer at each attempt. This went on for several years until the art of towing aloft was perfected and flights attaining over a thousand feet of altitude were achieved.

While the Australians were busy down under, the Southern California countryside was experiencing a hang gliding Renaissance of its own. Men like Volmer Jensen and Richard Miller were building uniquely designed flying craft, including in Miller's case, a bamboo and plastic Rogallo. These colorful gliders were characterized by a parallel bar cage suspended below the wing from which the pilot hung by his armpits. In flight control was accomplished by sliding around on the bars - not a very comfortable experience.

In 1969 the inevitable happened: the Australians came to America. Bill Bennett made a whirlwind exhibition tour of the country then settled in California and taught many eager students to fly. What followed immediately was a total exchange of technology. The Australian method of suspension and control, utilizing a seat and a triangular bar was quickly

3

adopted to replace the parallel bars (figure 3). The small gilders the Australians were towing (with spar lengths of 13 feet) required high flying speeds to lift an average size pilot. The larger American designs were found to be controllable, so the crafts grew larger and the flying speeds slowed down. What this change eventually led to was the fact that a pilot

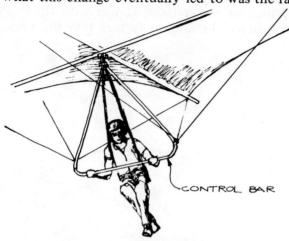

FIGURE 3.- CONTROL BAR

could run along, supporting his glider, until flying speed was achieved. At last, here was a design that could be launched, landed, carried and controlled all under the power of the pilot! This was something the public could appreciate. Soon manufacturers sprang up and homebuilders were cutting, drilling and splicing everywhere. By the early 70's, the sport had spread to the East and hillsides were decorated with the attention getting contraptions.

A whole new breed of pioneers appeared. These were the young experimenters, designers and pilots that carried the Rogallo concept far beyond the original format. A Californian, Dave Kilbourne, introduced soaring in a Rogallo to the world. In September, 1973, he rode the updrafts deflected by the slopes of Mission Peak for over an hour. Soon everyone was trying their hand at staying aloft. The limits of the design were explored through cut-and-try methods and mathematical analysis. Fly-ins and meets were popularized and became proving grounds for new ideas. The gliders that emerged were generally safer and out-performed the early models in every way.

Increased flight capabilities led to the use of ridge and thermal lift to reach incredible heights and travel amazing distances. Records were set and broken in every phase of the sport. At this point in time, hang glider pilots have remained aloft for over 15 hours, reached altitudes of over 19,000 feet (5,790M) and covered over 50 miles (80 KM). Flights lasting all day and extending over 100 miles are entirely possible. It is only a matter of the right combination of conditions, glider and pilot. The adventure in creative design and perfection of flight is still moving at a fast pace.

4

THE GLIDERS

The first pilots of Rogallo hang gliders used the basic design as pictured in figure 4. This is referred to as a "standard" glider. The names of the parts that are generally in use for all hang gliders are given. All pilots should become familiar with these terms.

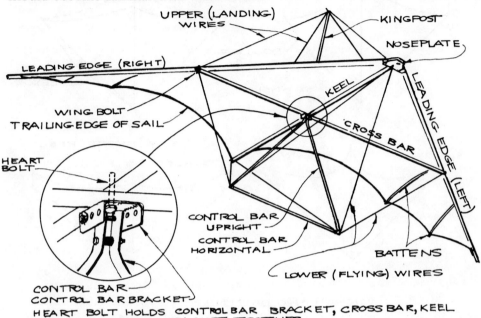

HEART BOLT HOLDS CONTROL BAR BRACKET, CROSS BAR, KEEL AND KINGPOST BRACKET TOGETHER

FIGURE 4.—TERMINOLOGY

The progressive changes in the Rogallo wing are pictured in figure 5. Besides the previously mentioned increase in size, the first commonly used design improvement was the shortened keel. Soon came the use of dog-leg and deflexors in early 1975. Dog-leg is an angle cut in the edge of a sail to compensate for the bending of the leading edges. Deflexors are outrigger-like cable supports to keep the leading edges from bending. Both of these additions helped prevent sail ripples and flutter. The next step was the hollow cutting of the trailing edge. This was followed by the use of truncated tips, improving slow speed flight characteristics. Further development led to the use of battens and roach. Roach is an extension of the sail beyond the normal limits of the spars. This extra material is made to hold its shape by inserting stiff battens into pockets sewn in the sail. The next addition was the double sail surface, or wide leading edge pocket. At the same time, curved (cambered) keels and J-wires appeared. This was accompanied by cambered leading edges and additional deflexors. In early 1976 radial battened tips were introduced. The use of battens for sail shaping became quite an art and allowed the sail to be stretched progressively tighter. Many other devices such as variable billow, raised keel pockets, curved battens and cambered sails appeared on successful designs.

5

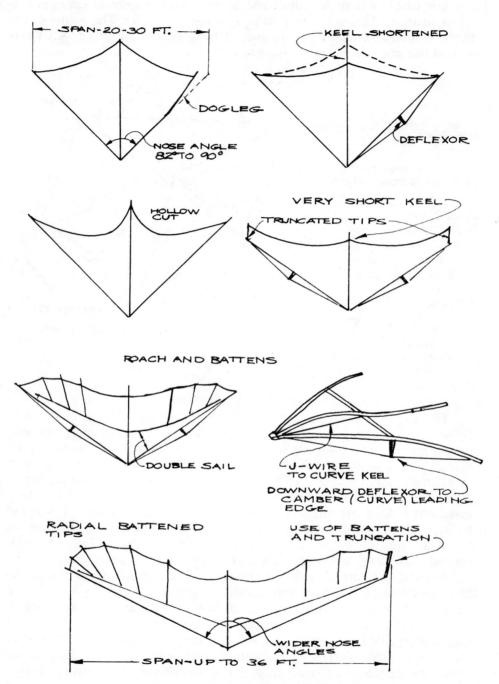

SPAN-20-30 FT.

DOGLEG

NOSE ANGLE
82° TO 90°

KEEL SHORTENED

DEFLEXOR

HOLLOW CUT

VERY SHORT KEEL

TRUNCATED TIPS

ROACH AND BATTENS

DOUBLE SAIL

J-WIRE
TO CURVE KEEL

DOWNWARD DEFLEXOR TO
CAMBER (CURVE) LEADING
EDGE

RADIAL BATTENED
TIPS

USE OF BATTENS
AND TRUNCATION

WIDER NOSE
ANGLES

SPAN-UP TO 36 FT.

FIGURE 5. — PROGRESSION OF DESIGN

6

Wider nose angles, wider control bars, wider span and greater structural strength brings the picture up to date. However, improvements are still being made and no one can predict a final result.

All this confusing array of rapidly changing designs meant one thing — improved performance. This, of course, was an important marketing factor. Subsequent chapters will examine the effects that each design change made on performance. The greatest benefit came from enhanced safety features. The new generation of hang gliders utilize sophisticated design elements to insure stability, dive recovery and quick response. The standard configuration does not necessarily possess these desirable features. In some areas, the standard gliders are being phased out for safety reasons. This does not mean that they are totally obsolete, but that their usefulness is limited. This matter is carried further in Chapter III.

Why didn't we have the advanced designs years ago? This question has probably been asked by every pilot that graduated from a standard to a newer design. The answer is limited designer know-how and pilot skill. These two factors are closely related. It took time for hang glider pilots to develop the flying expertise to handle the high performance craft. Likewise, it took time for the designer to digest the feedback information from the flyers and apply it to his own experience. If one of the super gliders that are flying today was introduced a few years back, it would have been rejected as too touchy or tricky to handle. One thing is sure: the intense market pressure will guarantee a continued search for the ultimate design. Lets hope it is light, small, strong, cheap and hungry for altitude.

CONSTRUCTION MATERIALS

Like any aircraft, a hang glider must be built with considerations for strength and weight, as well as flying ability. Although original designs were thrown together with "spit and shoe polish," modern gliders utilize aircraft hardware, strong aluminum tubing and sails of stabilized Dacron®.

Hardware consists of stainless steel cable, along with thimbles, Nico-presses and tangs used to fasten the cable to bolts, turnbuckles and shackles (see figure 6). All bolts must be made of hardened steel (grade 5 or better). These are loosely called AN bolts since aircraft quality bolts have a government numerical specification preceeded by the letters AN. To fasten the bolts, self-locking AN nuts (with plastic inserts to grip the bolt) or AN wing nuts with tempered safety pins are required. Turnbuckles are used to take up slack in a cable. Shackles usually appear as a connection devise between the lower wires and the control bar. Turnbuckles and shackles must meet aircraft or marine standards.

Aluminum tubing has a great strength to weight ratio, good corrosion resistance and flexibility. There are three types used in hang gliding: 2024-T3, 6061-T6, 6063-T832. The numbers refer to the alloy content and the method of heat treating. These three types vary in cost, weight, ultimate strength, elasticity and resistance to dents. All these are suitable for hang gliding construction and are the only grades of aluminum that should be used by anyone with less than a metallurgist's knowledge of material strengths.

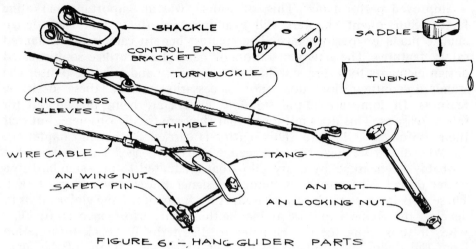

FIGURE 6. — HANG GLIDER PARTS

The sail material of almost every hang glider today is made of 3.8 oz. (per square yard) Dacron® Early experiments with plastic and Nylon® proved these materials unsatisfactory due to stretching, short lifetime or high porosity. Dacron® is strong with long-term durability and resistance to all chemicals except alkaline products (see Chapter VII on sail care). The beautiful dyes used in the synthetic material fairly glow when silhouetted against the sky. It is apparent that the designer must not only be an aerodynamicist but an aesthetic and structural engineer as well.

HANG GLIDING AND YOU

The progression of hang glider design and flight possibilities has been paralleled by an improvement in public awareness and organization of the sport. This can be detected in the subtle change of the news media from sensationalism to intelligent, inside reporting. It should be obvious that hang gliding has arrived as a respected form of recreational aviation. It is the realization of this fact that has brought about the concern for safety and upgrading of instruction methods. Indeed a hang glider is an aircraft requiring the same sort of controls and skills needed to safely pilot any other aircraft. The amount of knowledge needed to fly a hang glider is about the same as for conventional flying. Instead of learning the use of instruments, the hang gliding student must learn to use natural indicators and body sensations to monitor his flight. The airplane pilot maneuvers by precisely coordinating his stick and foot pedals. The hang glider pilot does the same with his control bar.

The dangers involved in hang gliding would be no greater than the dangers in any form of flying (which is statistically safer than driving an automobile), except for the matter of pilot maturity.

The most dangerous pilot is one flying for the fans. If friends or relatives are watching there is a great urge to perform. Sometimes this performance taxes the limits of ones skills. A mature pilot can resist this human tendency to show off. A pilot with the need to attract attention would do everyone a favor by joining a rock band.

In the past, hang gliders were available to anyone with no thought for proper training or guidance. This resulted in a large number of self taught and unskilled pilots. The excitement and sensational appeal of the sport led some to venture into conditions they could not handle. Others with insufficient knowledge of the design limitations of their craft went beyond the point of no return. This situation occured in every form of aviation when it first became popular. Fortunately, we have learned from our mistakes and have made available the knowledge necessary for safe and enjoyable flying.

The best way to acquire hang gliding knowledge is to attend a reputable school. Make sure the instructors are certified by the United States Hang Gliding Association (USHGA). This guarantees that the instructor has passed an extensive test of his teaching ability and understanding. Most hang gliding courses follow the USHGA Hang Rating Program. This program is designed to logically follow a pilot's learning from Hang I through Hang V. At each level of progress a card is received indicating pilot proficiency level. Completed tasks are signed off by official observers. The main purpose of the program is not to award achievement, but to guide a student in his training stages and insure safe flying at sites. With the Hang Rating system, a site director can be assured that a pilot can handle the conditions or unique problems presented by the hill. In the long run, each individual pilot is responsible for himself. In the air he is the only one making decisions concerning his flying. He must have the sense to learn the important skills and guidelines that make flying safe.

Get in touch with local clubs and other pilots. This is the best way to find out about flying sites and nearby activities. By all means, join the national organization and subscribe to as many publications as you can afford. There is a wealth of information in the hang gliding periodicals. Keep a log book detailing all your flights. This is a great learning device as it requires attention to the details of conditions and accomplishments. A log is a valuable aid in detecting problems on a long term basis and comes in handy when reminiscing with flying buddies.

Actually one of the greatest joys in hang gliding comes from joining someone in the air. There is nothing to compare with sharing the sky with a friend and perhaps a hawk or two. Across the gap that separates your wings there is an unspoken communication. Anyone who has flown a hang glider understands the feeling of total freedom. You become one with your wings and grace the surrounding air with fleeting traces of expressive delight. Hang gliding introduces you to an entirely new environment, leaving worldly cares far below. The possibilities for adventure are unlimited. The rewards are total enjoyment and a chance to really fly!

9

CHAPTER II

WHY IT FLIES

Aerodynamics is the study of forces on a body moving through the air. A knowledge of basic aerodynamics is important in order to fully comprehend how to control and maximize performance in a glider. By understanding the forces at work on our wings we can take the mystery out of flight and appreciate the potentials of the sport. Part of the fun that comes along with the whole flying experience is learning how to apply ideas and explanations to situations encountered in the air. To be a good pilot you must know what's happening at all times.

This chapter is written for the beginning student. The explanations are simplified so that the reader can easily grasp the important ideas. Chapter VI investigates the subject of aerodynamics in much greater depth and relates to matters important to more advanced flyers.

THE AIRFOIL

All flying surfaces have a peculiar shape which allows them to generate a lifting force when moving throught the air. A surface with this property is called an airfoil. Figure 7 depicts some well-known airfoils found in nature and man's copy — the airplane wing. The shaded cross sections

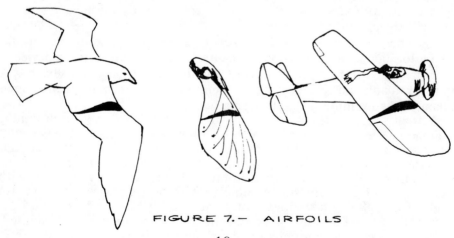

FIGURE 7.— AIRFOILS

indicate that the flying surfaces are curved on top and more or less straight on the bottom. Why does this make the wing fly? First, imagine a section of an airfoil with a wind blowing across it as in figure 8. The air

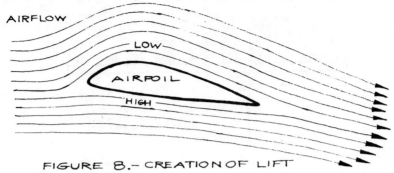

FIGURE 8.— CREATION OF LIFT

is assumed to be smooth (laminar) and reaches the wing in an orderly fashion. The air moving over the top of the wing must follow a curved path, and therefore, has farther to travel than the air moving under the wing. In a sense, the air over the top is stretched and the molecules are spread out. This results in a reduction of pressure on the upper surface since pressure from a gas is related to how many molecules per unit volume are present. The purpose of an airfoil is to disturb the air in such a way that a relative high pressure area is created below the wing and a low on top.

The distribution of the pressure on a typical airfoil is shown in figure 9. Note that the pressure increases as the airfoil meets the air at a greater angle. This angle (α) is called the angle of attack. It is the measured

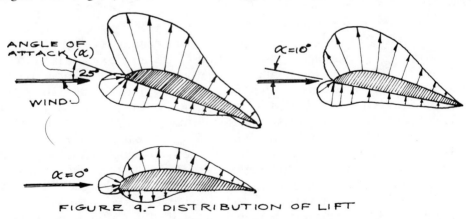

FIGURE 9.— DISTRIBUTION OF LIFT

angle between the wind striking the airfoil and the chord. The chord of an airfoil is the straight line drawn from the furthest forward point (leading edge) to the point furthest back (trailing edge) on the wing.

All the forces represented by the arrows in figure 9 can be added together and considered to be acting at one point called the "center of pressure" (C.P.). This is similar to the way the forces exerted by a group

11

of unequal weights on a beam can balance as if they were all acting at one point (see figure 10). We will identify the combined upward forces on a wing as the lifting force, or simply "lift" (see figure 11).

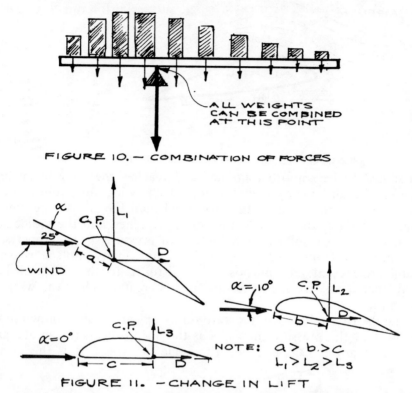

FIGURE 10. — COMBINATION OF FORCES

FIGURE 11. — CHANGE IN LIFT

For this gift of lift we pay a penalty. This penalty is called drag. Drag is a force always parallel to the direction of the air flow. The lift force is always represented perpendicular to the drag force. The total drag (D) can be separated into two parts: the profile drag (Dp) and induced drag (Di). Profile drag is due to the viscosity or stickiness of the air. In a very viscous fluid, such as molasses, it is easy to imagine a great amount of profile drag. The cause of this in any fluid is the fact that even the smoothest glass has great surface irregularities on the microscopic level which trap and tumble the molecules moving over it. This slows the fluid next to the surface resulting in a force tending to drag the surface along with the flow of the fluid. In a flying craft, all solid objects exposed to the moving air create "parasitic" drag which is included with the profile drag. Induced drag is caused by the fact that when the air exerts a lifting force on the wing, the wing exerts an equal and opposite force on the air. This deflects the air downward at the rear of the wing, creating turbulence and vortices. The energy that imparts this swirling motion to the air in the wake of the wing comes from the momentum of the wing itself. This energy loss tends to slow the wing down and is represented as induced drag.

12

Most hang gliders utilize a peculiar airfoil. This is a single surface membrane which takes the characteristic curved shape. Figure 12 illustrates this by showing a cross section of the sail cut by a vertical plane parallel to the direction of flight. The single surface airfoil operates under

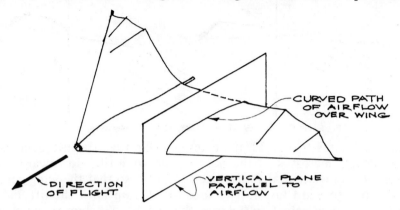

FIGURE 12 .— HANG GLIDER AIRFOIL

the same principles as the conventional double surface airfoil. It is somewhat less efficient in most respects. However, the general stability, lift, weight and ability to be folded make the membrane wing ideal for popular hang gliding.

THE FLYING WING

Up to now we have been considering a stationary airfoil with the air blowing into it or a wing being forced through the air. The foregoing discussion is fine for the wing of a powered airplane, but what about non-powered wings such as the maple seed or a hang glider? In these cases we must alter our position slightly. For one thing, we must understand what makes a glider move forward into the wind. The truth is, all flying objects without power get their energy from gravity. A glider simply converts some of its downward, falling motion (due to gravity) to forward motion. It does this by being slightly tilted so that air escapes to the rear of the wing. You may recall from high school physics the well-worn statement: "for every action there is an equal and opposite reaction". Well, Newton was right; in this case, the momentum of the air moving backwards imparts an equal momentum to the wing in the forward direction. An easy way to illustrate this is to construct a paper airplane and release it in a level position without a push. The nose will drop slightly, then the model will pick up speed and fly away. Figure 13(a) shows the balance of forces on a glider. The force of gravity is represented by the weight (W). This is always balanced in steady flight by the sum of the forces of lift and drag called the resultant (R). If W is not balanced by R, as in figure 13(b), the glider will accelerate until both the lift and drag increase to the point of reinstating the equilibrium.

From this analysis, it is easy to see how a gilder changes flying speed.

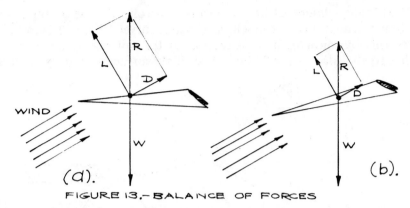

FIGURE 13.—BALANCE OF FORCES

Looking at figures 9 and 11 it becomes clear that the lift decreases as angle of attack decreases. If the nose of the wing tilts downward the lift decreases. This means that R has been reduced so that the wing begins to fall and move forward faster. The speed builds up until the lift and drag forces take on new values to balance the weight. To slow the wing down the opposite must occur — angle of attack and hence, lift must increase. The important thing to remember is that flying speed varies **only** with angle of attack for a given glider and flying weight.

It is interesting to note how the drag changes. The profile drag decreases as velocity decreases, which relates to a higher angle of attack. The induced drag increases as the angle of attack increases. Therefore, starting at dive speed, the total drag (sum of Dp and Di) will decrease to a point, then increase rapidly as angle of attack increases and velocity decreases. Chapter VI will cover this in greater depth.

GLIDER CONTROL AND STALLS

How do we change angle of attack in a hang glider? Most hang gliders control by weight shift only. The pilot is suspended from the glider by a harness and he holds onto a control bar as in figure 14 (a). In constant flight the pilot's weight is directly under the center of pressure. If the pilot pushes on the control bar his weight shifts back slightly (exaggerated in 14 (b)). This means the resultant force and the weight force are no longer in line. A rotation force is created that lifts the nose of the wing, increases the angle of attack and thus, slows the glider down (14c). To speed up the pilot simply pulls in on the bar.

It would seem that the pilot could continue pushing out and make the glider fly slower and slower to spend more time in the air. Unfortunately, this is not so. Every conventional flying device has a maximum usable angle of attack called the "stall point". Beyond this point there is a sudden loss of lift and control. A "stall". occurs because of the air's inability to make sudden changes in velocity. The air has mass. Therefore it wants to continue traveling in its initial direction due to inertia. In figure 15 we see what happens at high angles of attack. The air can no

14

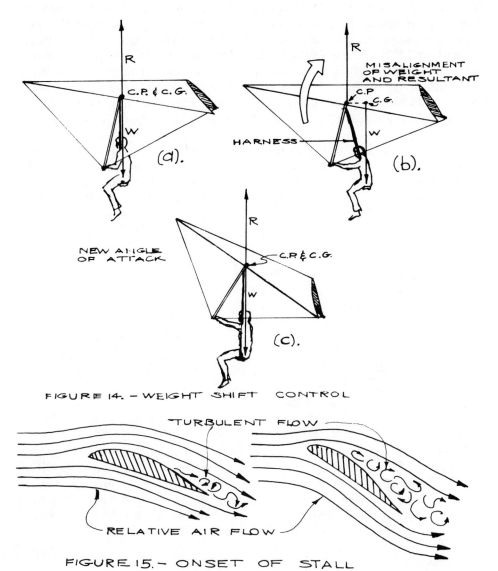

FIGURE 14. - WEIGHT SHIFT CONTROL

FIGURE 15. - ONSET OF STALL

longer make the sudden change to flow smoothly over the upper surface. It breaks away at the rear and creates turbulence, increasing the drag considerably. If the nose is raised higher the point of break-away moves forward and a sudden loss of lift occurs. What happens then is usually a steep dive (due to excessive drag forces on the rear of the wing) and then a return to normal flight after lift again developes. If the pilot continues to push out, a stall will again occur followed by a dive. A paper airplane can be made to simulate this action by weighting the tail. The danger of a stall lies in the fact that it may take 50 or more feet (16M) of altitude to

15

recover. This distance is covered quickly in a dive. In addition, the pilot has little directional control during a stall and cannot avoid obstacles. Learning to recognize and avoid a stall while flying is one of the most basic skills learned in hang gliding. Hang glider stall speeds vary between 14 and 18 MPH (22-29 KPH). It should be clear that the stall speed determines the minimum flying speed of the glider since it relates to the maximum angle of attack. Thus, the minimum take-off and landing speed depends on the speed at which stall occurs. This is an important concept to hang gliding since take-offs and landings are made on the fleet feet of the pilot.

The nose-up and nose-down movement of the glider is referred to as "pitch control". There are two other control directions we must consider as pictured in figure 16. Yaw is a movement of one wing forward or a rotation about a vertical axis. This is not of great importance in a glider

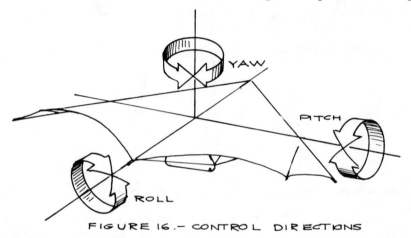

FIGURE 16.— CONTROL DIRECTIONS

designed for beginners and will be treated in a later chapter. Roll is a dipping of one wing, or rotation about a horizontal axis. A turn is initiated by rolling the glider to one side. Roll control is accomplished in much the same way as pitch control. In figure 17 we see a pilot has pushed himself to the left side of the control bar. This means his weight is directed to the left of the resultant. The glider will then roll to the left.

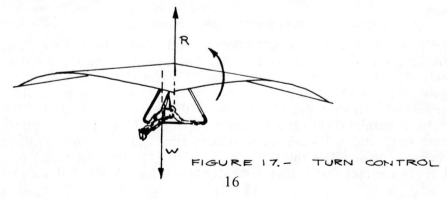

FIGURE 17.— TURN CONTROL

16

STABILITY

Stability is the tendency for a glider to return to normal level flight whether it is dived, stalled, rolled or yawed. A glider that is "in trim" should fly a few miles an hour faster than stall speed with no control force from the pilot at all. In the case of pitch stability, this means that a glider in a dive should have a strong tendency to slow up. A glider near a stall should want to speed up. If we look again at figure 9 and 11 we see that along with the change in magnitude of the lift force, the position of the center of pressure on an airfoil changes with angles of attack. In general, the C.P. will move forward as the angle of attack increases and back as the angle decreases. The center of gravity remains in the same place since the attachment point of the pilot does not move. Consequently, we have the situation depicted in figure 18. Here we see at high angle of attack the tendency is for the wing to nose up even more and to nose down even

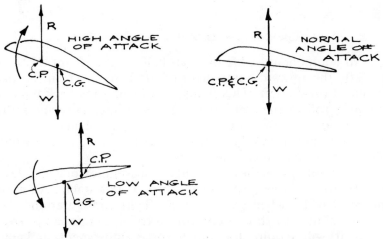

FIGURE 18. — CHANGE IN C. P. POSITION

more at low angle of attack. Not exactly a desirable state of affairs! The truth is, all airfoils as we have pictured them have this unwanted trait called divergence or instability.

These are several ways to overcome the problem. First, we can add reflex to the airfoil. Reflex is an upward curving of the rear of the wing. In a hang glider this is accomplished by upcurving the tail of the keel. What this does is destroy lift at the tail at high speeds so that the nose of the glider wants to pull up and thus slow the craft down. Another way to provide pitch stability is to design the entire aircraft so that lifting surfaces that are behind the center of gravity lose lift quicker than areas that are ahead of the C.G. This means that more lift will be forward at high speeds to pull the nose up, and more lift will be at the rear at low speeds to force the nose down. Airplanes utilize the tail section (elevator) in this manner. Hang gliders use this idea by varying the lift on the tips which are swept behind the C.G. Most hang gliders use a combination of these

17

techniques. All standards must have reflex to be stable. Without reflex they are liable to dive uncontrollably. Chapter III details how to check for proper reflex.

Stability in roll is effected through dihedral. Dihedral is taken to mean an upward tilting of the wings, like the wings of a pigeon in flight. Figure 19 shows the rear view of a wing with (exaggerated) dihedral. Note the

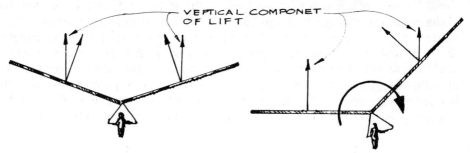

VERTICAL COMPONET OF LIFT

FIGURE 19.— STABILITY IN ROLL

upward component of lift on each half in level flight. If the wing rolls to the left, the upward component of lift is reduced on the right wing and enhanced on the left. This tends to roll the wing back to center or equilibrium. A roll to the right creates a similar imbalance and return to center. Yaw stability is accomplished in an identical manner except that the forces are drag forces and sweep (rearward angle of the wings) instead of dihedral is what changes the forces.

The whole problem of stability is a complex one and deserves a lot of our attention. A design is not safe if it is not stable. An unstable aircraft will react widly when put in certain flight configurations. This overtaxes a pilot's ability to stay in control. In truth, a craft can be overstable. This means it will require too much force (movement in hang gliding) to change speeds or roll. Designers spend many hours calculating and testing to come up with the right combinations to follow the thin line between stability and instability.

HANG GLIDER PERFORMANCE

When we speak of the performance of a glider we speak of many things, including how it handles, how fast or how far it flies and how slow it descends. More specifically, we want to know its roll and pitch response, speed range, glide ratio and sink rate.

Roll response or roll rate is a measure of how quickly the glider reacts to the pilot's side to side movements. A good roll rate is necessary so that the pilot can turn and maneuver quickly. Ways to improve the roll rate are numerous. Reducing the weight or amount of flying surface at the tips, adding a raised keel pocket, reducing dihedral or combining these design parameters proves effective. Note that reducing dihedral reduces stability.

Pitch response depends on keel length and other, more complex

18

factors. This will be delt with in more detail in Chapter VI. It should be easy to see that both pitch and roll response depend on the pilot's weight compared to the size of the glider. The smaller the glider is, the more effect the pilot's weight shift will have.

The speed range also depends on pilot weight. The heavier a pilot is for a particular glider, the faster will be his maximum speed capabilities. The reason for this is that flying speed is developed from the force of gravity. A heavier pilot creates a greater downward force on the glider. The shape of the sail and the wings also affect maximum speed. For a Hang glider this varies between 35 and 60 MPH (56-96 KPH). The slowest possible speed is determined by the stall point. Recall that a glider stalls at a given angle of attack. A heavier pilot will be flying faster at this stall angle of attack and therefore has a higher minimum speed than a lighter pilot. The shape of the airfoil is the big factor in determining the stall angle of attack.

The glide ratio and sink rate are two of the most useful concepts when describing a glider's performance. Briefly, the glide ratio is the ratio of how far a glider will travel horizontally for every unit of distance it drops in the vertical direction (see figure 20). Most flexible wing hang gliders

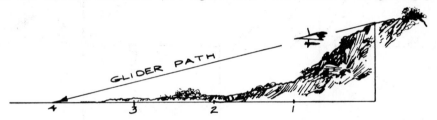

FIGURE 20. — EXAMPLE OF 4/1 GLIDE RATIO

have a maximum glide ratio from 4/1 (for standards) to 10/1. It is desireable to have a high maximum glide ratio in order to fly further. Figure 37 indicates how the glide path varies as the maximum glide ratio of the glider increases. A 4/1 glide ratio will allow the pilot to fly four times the take-off height away from the hill. With a 6/1 glide ratio, the pilot can fly 1½ times further. Note how the angle with the horizontal is reduced as glide ratio is increased. If you know your glider's maximum glide ratio, you can measure this angle with a protractor and determine whether or not you can reach a landing field by measuring the angle between the field and the take-off.

The sink rate is simply the speed at which the glider travels downward. Sink rate should be minimized so that the glider stays in the air longer. The exact relationship between glide ratio, sink rate and flying speed must be understood in order for a pilot to fly where he wants to and get the most out of his flights. In figure 21 we see a hang glider in flight with the principle forces and velocities indicated. Note that several angles of attack are illustrated. Study the drawing to get an idea how the forces and velocities change at different angles of attack. The arrows representing lift, drag, weight and the resultant should be familiar. The arrow (vector) labeled V represents the direction and magnitude of the flying velocity. Vh is the component of velocity in the horizontal directon and Vv is the component in the vertical direction.

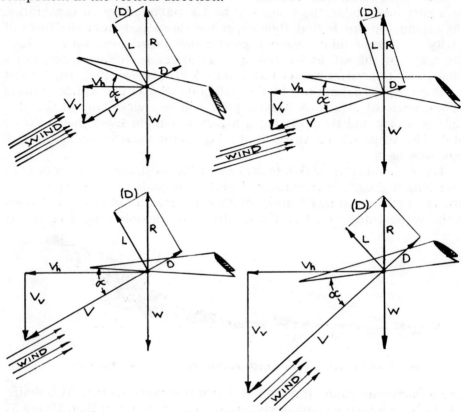

FIGURE 21. — VELOCITY CHANGE

Immediately, we can make several observations. First, the direction of the air hitting the glider is directly opposite the velocity, V. This is true in a wind from any direction or in complete calm. For example, if a breeze is blowing from behind the glider, the glider simply moves along faster but has the same angle of attack with respect to the wind. The velocity will always be the same through the air at a given angle of attack. Remember that a glider gets energy to move through the air from gravity, not the air itself. The wind the glider "sees" is called the "relative wind". The relative wind is parallel to V, so the angle of attack (∝) can be measured between V and the chord of the wing.

The next thing to note is that the sink rate is identified with the vertical component of velocity Vv. To minimize the sink rate we must minimize Vv. In addition, we can see that the glide ratio (horizontal distance divided by vertical distance) is equal to Vh/Vv. This is true because

20

distance traveled is proportional to the velocity of travel. Thus, to maximize the glide ratio we need to maximize Vh and minimize Vv. Note further that the drag force (D) is always directed opposite the velocity. Also the lift force (L) is always perpendicular to the drag force and the direction of flight. Consequently, by applying simple rules of geometry we can see that the triangle with sides defined by R, L and (D) is similar to (has the same angles and proportions) the triangle defined by V, Vh, and Vv. Therefore, the ratio L/D equals Vh/Vv, which is, of course, the glide ratio. This is why advertisements and pilots make mention of a glider's maximum L/D. They are speaking of the best glide capabilities of the craft. It is clear that maximizing glide ratio requires as much lift and as little drag as possible. This has been the main interest of designers since the nature of these forces became known.

The important thing for a pilot to learn is how to fly his glider at the different speeds which correspond to the stall point, best sink rate (Vvmin) and best glide ratio (L/D max). The stall point is of course the slowest speed attainable. It is not readily apparent that the min. sink speed is not the L/D max. speed. The speed to fly for min. sink is below 20 MPH (32 KPH) for a hang glider, while the L/D max. speed is 3 to 5 MPH (4.8-8 KPH) faster. Figure 22 explains the difference. The picture shows

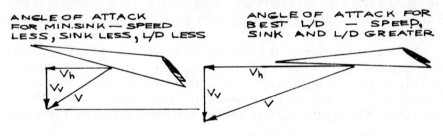

ANGLE OF ATTACK FOR MIN.SINK — SPEED LESS, SINK LESS, L/D LESS

ANGLE OF ATTACK FOR BEST L/D — SPEED, SINK AND L/D GREATER

FIGURE 22.— MIN. SINK AND BEST GLIDE

two identical gliders at different angles of attack and thus, different speeds (the length of V is proportional to speed). The first glider is flying at the speed for best glide ratio; the second at min. sink speed. Note that the first glider has a higher ratio of Vh to Vv or L to D. The second glider has the smallest value of Vv. If the two gliders took off at the same time, their flights would appear as in figure 23. Here we see the gliders in various stages of their flights. The glider flying L/D max. follows the upper path. The glider flying min. sink follows the lower path. After 10 seconds the gliders are at B and B'; after 20 seconds at C and C'; after 30 seconds they are at D and D'. Note that the L/D max. flyer has landed after 30 seconds while the min. sink flyer is still in the air. This is because the L/D max flyer travels faster. The conclusion is a glider flown at L/D max. speed will go further, while the same glider flown at min. sink speed will stay in the air longer. The importance of this concept during competition or varying conditions is obvious. Any speed faster or slower than L/D max. speed will result in a poorer glide ratio, while any speed faster or slower than min. sink speed will result in less time in the air.

There is one case when the glide ratio is better than L/D max. This is in ground effect. Ground effect is the apparent floating near the ground as

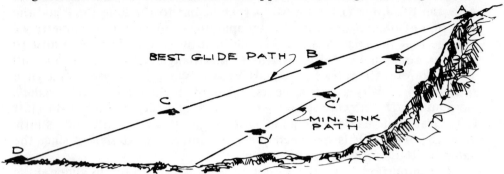

FIGURE 23. – DIFFERENCE IN MIN. SINK AND BEST GLIDE

if the glider was on a "cushion of air". There may indeed be a small amount of cushioning between the wing and the ground, but the major cause of ground effect is the reduction of wing tip vorticies. Wing tip vortices are swirls of air at the tips of any flying surface. They are caused by air moving rearward and outward along a wing, then rolling over the top. You can simulate this by running your hand through the water in a bath tub. See the swirls?

A large percentage of the drag on a kite represents the energy used up in creating wing tip vorticies. They are directly related to the induced drag so that at slow flying speeds (e.g. during landing) when induced drag is highest, the vorticies will be strongest. In figure 24 we see how the ground can cancel the negative effect of the vorticies by cutting them off. The

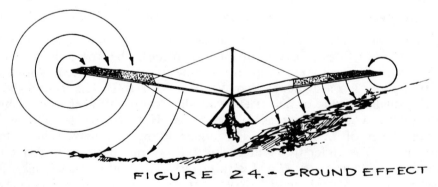

FIGURE 24. – GROUND EFFECT

wing on the right will achieve a much better L/D. Ground effect begins at about a wing span from the ground and becomes more pronounced the lower one gets. Ground effect certainly helps a little on take-off. On landing the glider seems to want to float forever.

SUMMARY

After reading this chapter on basic aerodynamics, the reader should be aware that many things are involved in optimizing our flight capabilities. In truth a hang glider is simply a pilot launchable airplane and as such obeys the same principles of flight that any flying craft adheres to. A student encountering this material for the first time may not be able to grasp all the ideas in depth, but this will not necessarily hamper his progress up to a point. After spending time in the air, listening intently to experienced pilots and asking many questions, reread any difficult parts and new insight will be gained. An advanced pilot certainly needs to know this material thoroughly.

A beginner should be aware of the following: a stall occurs at the minimum flying speed. To avoid stalls, simply avoid flying too slowly. Reflex is absolutely necessary on all beginning gliders. A standard glider without reflex will be unsafe at high speeds. The speeds to fly for best L/D and minimum sink are completely different. These speeds should be learned for the glider the pilot is using (they vary with design) by varying the flying speed and noting the effects. Remember that all speeds (stall speed, min. sink speed, L/D max. speed, top speed) increase on a given glider as pilot weight increases. Armed with this basic knowledge, a beginner can safely progress through the first lessons — well on his way to totally controlled free flight. The skys await your presence.

CHAPTER III

SELECTING YOUR EQUIPMENT

If you are learning the art of hang gliding by attending a school, you can obtain guidance from your instructor when ready to buy your own equipment. This chapter will be a source of reference, preparing you to ask meaningful questions. If you are about to obtain hang gliding equipment without the advise of an expert, then study this chapter well and take the time to apply each point to your prospective purchase. Experience has shown that the most important factor in learning hang gliding is having the proper equipment.

THE GLIDER

The things to consider when buying a glider are the design, size, weight, condition and cost. The design will usually determine all the other factors. The higher performance a particular design is, the smaller the glider has to be for a given pilot weight, the more it weighs due to added structure and the more it costs. Let us look at the general designs available to determine the best all-around glider for a beginner.

Years ago all pilots learned to fly on "standard" rogallos since this was the only design available. These gliders had a nose angle from 82° to 90° and equal length spars (keel and leading edges). Their performance was quite low. Today there is no major manufacturer producing a glider of this design, but used "standards" are available. A "standard" is acceptable for training, but many areas and organizations are banning these gliders due to possible dive recovery problems. If you decide to buy a "standard" be aware that you may not be able to fly it at all sites. Furthermore, within a few months you will be yearning for a better performing glider to fly longer and further. Glider designs with no battens and shortened keels fall into the same category as "standards".

An "advanced standard" or intermediate glider incorporates battens, roach, deflexors and a shortened keel (see Chapter I). Performance is considerably improved. Take-offs are a bit easier than with the "standard", pitch control is a little quicker and landings somewhat more difficult. They will not parachute (float down at a steep glide) as well as a "standard" and must have more landing room. This design is highly recommended for beginners.

High performance gliders are much greater in span with tighter sails, wider nose angles and usually incorporate more battens than the intermediates. A beginner can certainly learn to fly on them but only under close surveillance from an instructor until advanced skills are learned. Most pilots couldn't afford to retain an instructor that long. The problem with high performance gliders is that they are harder to control in roll and yaw although they are more stable than other designs. In addition, they require considerable practice in order to perfect a well timed and well placed landing. A beginner will have a hard time on landing which could prove discouraging or even dangerous.

The size of the glider is a major consideration. If a glider is too big for a pilot he will have trouble controlling the glider on the ground prior to take off and even greater trouble in the air when trying to turn or penetrate a wind. If a glider is too small, the minimum flying speed will be faster than the pilot can run. Each glider has an optimum weight range according to design and size. This weight range is determined by the "wing loading", which is the ratio of the weight of the pilot and glider to the sail area. Wing loading is expressed in pounds per square feet. The higher the performance of the glider, the higher the wing loading should be (it flies more efficiently) and greater is the range of safe pilot weights.

A good indicator of performance or efficiency is the aspect ratio (AR) This is explained in Chapter VII, but for now we can use the AR to determine glider size. The charts in figure 25 provide the information regarding what size glider to buy. Simply locate the aspect ratio of the glider under

ASPECT RATIO	2.6	2.8	3.0	3.5	4.0	4.5	5.0
WING LOADING	.8-1.0	.8-1.0	.85-1.05	.85-1.1	.9-1.2	.95-1.3	1-1.4

SAIL AREA

	140	150	160	170	180	190	200	210	220	230	250	270
.8	112	120	128	136	144	152	160	168	176	184	200	216
.85	119	127.5	136	144.5	153	161.5	170	178.5	187	195.5	212.5	229.5
.9	126	135	144	153	162	171	180	189	198	207	225	243
.95	133	142.5	152	161.5	171	180.5	190	199.5	209	218.5	237.5	256.5
1.0	140	150	160	170	180	190	200	210	220	230	250	270
1.05	147	157.5	168	178.5	189	199.5	210	220.5	231	241.5	262.5	283.5
1.1	154	165	176	187	198	209	220	231	242	253	275	297
1.2	168	180	192	204	216	228	240	252	264	276	300	324
1.3	182	195	208	221	234	247	260	273	286	299	325	351
1.4	196	210	224	238	252	266	280	294	308	322	350	378

FIGURE 25. — GLIDER SIZE CHART

consideration in the first chart and note the wing loading range below. Go to the second chart and find the sail area along the top. Follow this column down to the interval given by the wing loading along the left side. The numbers in the interval are the recommended values of the combined glider and pilot weight. Subtract the weight of the glider from these

25

combined weights and you will find what your weight should be for a given glider.

The weights given here are for zero wind. As the wind velocity increases higher wing loadings are in order since gust strength increases with wind velocity and higher wing loadings provide more control. To correct the weights given for the effect of wind, simply move down the weight column one place for every 10 MPH wind.

The following example illustrates the method of checking a glider to see if it is appropriate for your weight. Suppose the glider in question has an aspect ratio of 3.5, a sail area of 210 sq. ft. and weighs 40 lbs. Furthermore, assume that you weight 150 lbs. fully dressed. From the first chart we see that your wing loading can be from .85 to 1.1 pounds per square foot. On the second chart we find the column under the 210 square feet of sail area and proceed downward until we find the interval from 178.5 to 231 lbs. which corresponds to the wing loading interval on the left side of the chart. Subtracting the glider weight from this interval gives the possible weights for this glider as 138.5 to 191 lbs. Note that you are at the lower limit of this glider's weight range and in a 10 MPH wind you would have the lightest wing loading advisable.

How do you find a glider's aspect ratio and sail area? The aspect ratio can be found by using the formula: $AR = (span)^2 / sail area$. An 82° nose "standard" has an AR of 2.6 and a sail area of $.656 \times (leading\ edge)^2$. A 90 nose "standard" has an AR of 2.8 and a sail area of $.707 \times (leading\ edge)^2$. If the sail area of other gliders is not known, contact a dealer or the manufacturer of the glider. Of course, these businesses can give you direct information concerning the proper weights for their gliders, but the charts provide insight into how this is derived.

The weight of the glider can be found by using a bathroom scales. Typical weights are from 30 to 40 lbs. (13.6 to 18.1 KG) for "standards" and 37 to 45 lbs. (16.80 to 20.41 KG) for intermediate gliders. High performance gliders usually weigh even more. Longer leading edges, larger tubing, deflexors and battens account for the extra weight. The heavier the glider the harder it will be to carry around. This can mean fewer flights when learning. You'll simply be more exhausted. In addition, you have more weight to hold up while taking off and more weight to throw around while flying. This point is of special importance to women and men with light builds. Obviously you want the lightest glider you can find, but it is usually necessary to put up with extra weight in order to get better performance and a solid structure.

The condition of the glider should receive special attention. It obviously must be sound since you will be suspended from it. A thorough check consists of the following: (1) Inspect all bolts for rust, straightness or wear. (2) Inspect all tubes for dents and straightness. (3) Inspect all cables for frays and rust. If the cable is uncoated, twist the wires to open the strands and examine the insides. (4) Set the glider up and sight down the crossbar. This should be nearly straight. Inspect the keel for the proper amount of reflex. There are two good ways to do this. One method is to draw a string taut along the top of the keel, fastening it at the nose and tail. Measure the distance between the string and the top of the keel at a point midway along the keel. This distance will be exactly half the amount of reflex. The other method is to have a friend assist you by holding a stick vertically beside the keel at the tail. He uses the finger of his free hand as a marker while you sight from the top of the nose plate along the bottom of the king post bracket to the stick. Have him move his finger until it is in the line of sight. The amount of reflex will be equal to the distance between his finger and the top of the keel. With practice you will be able to closely estimate reflex by simply sighting down the keel. Be sure that the front-to-back wires top and bottom are tight or you will not be measuring the true reflex. In flight the lower wires are always tight, so the true (flying) reflex can only be measured if the upper wires are tightened to hold the ends of the keel up while you sight down it. Remember that early Rogallos did not even have a kingpost and upper wires, yet still had reflex in flight, determined by the length of the lower wires. Do not confuse this point. (5) Inspect the sail for abrasions and tears. Sails on "standard" gliders loose their stiffness very rapidly due to their tendency to flap. This makes them more porous and causes increased flapping. An experienced pilot can tell the condition of a sail by feeling it. Be sure the sail is sewn with a zig-zag stitch, otherwise, the seams will not stretch with the rest of the sail. You should watch the glider in flight and see how the sail behaves. Massive wrinkles occuring across the whole sail mean the sail has stretched. These wrinkles are very hard to remove and hurt performance. A little bit of flutter on a used glider should be expected.

If any of the above parts are found to be defective, replacement is necessary. You must figure in these costs when bargaining for a used glider. Remember, most manufacturers employ pilots who rarely keep a glider longer than a few months. They don't necessarily know how much wear occurs in normal use. It is up to you to find the problems. Common things to look for are leading edges bent at the cross bar attachment, thimbles pulled out from the cables, bent heart bolts, and cables that have stretched so much that tightening the turnbuckles doesn't take out all the slack. Of course, the previous owner has a lot to do with the condition of the glider. Buy from a careful and honest individual.

The last thing to consider is the price. "Standard" gliders are cheap. You should never pay more than a few hundred dollars for a used "standard". Never buy a new one since they have a very low resale value and you'll soon be tired of it. There are many used intermediate gliders entering the market. These will be more expensive, but well worth the price. The best policy a beginner can follow is to buy a used intefmediate glider, learn to fly and develop skills for a year, then move up to an advanced glider. This proceedure will greatly minimize cost. If you prefer new equipment or will be only flying occasionally, purchase a new glider, take care of it and it will take you for joy rides for many years to come. If you follow these guidelines, get a good deal and find your favorite colors in the process, you will be on top of the world indeed.

BUILDING YOUR OWN

There are many reasons why a person would want to build his own glider. These include the sense of accomplishment this can provide and the desire to save on costs. At this point, however, it is advisable not to construct your own unless you have a bit of aircraft building experience. The reason for this is that the gliders of today are very refined with many subtleties and unless you know what you're doing you'll end up with a very poor performing or unsafe glider. A few years back many plans were available for the fabrication of "standard" gliders, but they perform so poorly that it isn't worth the effort.

Many homebuilders find that the cost savings isn't too great, especially considering the fact that the manufacturers buy expensive aircraft hardware in large quantities and thus get a sizeable price break. If you really have an urge to build your own, learn to fly and get familiar with all the complications involved before you start to work. You will save yourself a lot of dissapointment.

In the interest of safety a few tips are included here to assist homebuilders.

(1) Make sure all Nico presses are compressed the proper amount. Use **only** a tool made specifically for this job. If pressed too much the Nico can damage the wire. If not pressed enough the wire will not be held firmly and your glider will fall apart in the air. If your wire cables are plastic coated you **must** remove the plastic before using Nicos. Use small vise grips to hold the wire on the thimble while you compress the Nicos. Get the Nico to hold tight against the thimble. Use a second Nico to hold the free end of the wire (see figure 6).

(2) Take your time to make all cables exact. As little as 1/8 of an inch difference in the lower cables can cause a noticeable bending to one side in the keel.

(3) Set the glider upside down and use wood blocks to hold the proper reflex when rigging the lower wires.

(4) When splicing tubing, be sure that the spar inserts at least three tube diameters into the sleeve (see figure 26).

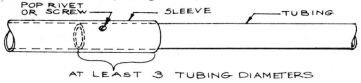

FIGURE 26. - SLEEVES

(5) Set up a jig to use with a drill press so that holes are drilled exactly in line. A dowel sunk in a piece of board will suffice.

(6) Use a light oil on the tube when inserting it in a sleeve. The smallest

amount of filings can jam the sleeve, making it impossible to move. Wipe this oil completely off the exposed portion of the tube as it will create a noticeable blotch on the sail. Never use graphite to lubricate or mark tubes. Graphite is known to deteriorate aluminum in the presence of vibrations.

(7) When applying bushings with a flare tool, be careful not to hammer too hard and deform the tube. Be sure to use a bushing that fits the bolt closely to prevent the tubes from twisting in flight.

(8) When sewing the sail be sure to use a zig-zag stitch so that the seam can stretch along with the rest of the sail.

(9) Use only AN materials. Hardware stores do not carry the necessary parts. You must locate aircraft suppliers.

Take great care in your construction and you will have many safe flights. Cut corners in the interest of saving time and money and you may not live to regret it.

THE HARNESS

Harnesses come in three basic types: prone, seated and supine. With a prone harness you fly lying down like Superman. Birds fly prone. With a seat harness you are sitting upright and have a different view of things. A supine harness lets the pilot lie on his back and really get comfortable.

Learning to fly prone is recommended. The reasons for this are: it is a lot easier to hold the glider with the harness straps tight, the harness does not hinder running and the body can be held off the ground while the glider runs along on the wheels in the case of an unsuccessful take-off. The drawback of learning prone is that it may feel like an unatural position to the beginner and he may not be able to immediately orientate his controls. This problem can be overcome by lengthening the attattchment straps so that the body only has to tilt at a 45° angle. The straps can be gradually shortened so that the body lies flat after a few weeks of flying. Another problem related to the prone position is the necessity to hold the head up for hours on some flights. This is of course, of little concern to beginners.

There are two basic types of prone harness shown in figure 27. All beginners should use the basic prone harness without knee hangers (attachments to the knees) to begin with. If your instructor starts you out using knee hangers, request that he remove them. They are not necessary for a beginner and make learning much more difficult. After you learn to consistently take off and fly level you can try using knee hangers — they hold your legs up in good form. To adjust knee hangers simply shorten the shoulder to leg line until your whole body lies flat while suspended. If you get the line too short, the knee hangers will impair running.

The full body harness doesn't have the secure holding and freedom necessary for learning. You can probably buy the basic prone harness used, at a considerable savings. Make sure that it fits comfortably (they are usually adjustable) and is not worn. The support straps (risers) bear most of your weight and should be inspected carefully. Look for loose or damaged threads. Make sure the waist strap is well padded. The leg straps

29

should be adjustable so that the waist strap is held down to the pelvic region. Otherwise, the harness will slip up and you will not be able to lie fully prone.

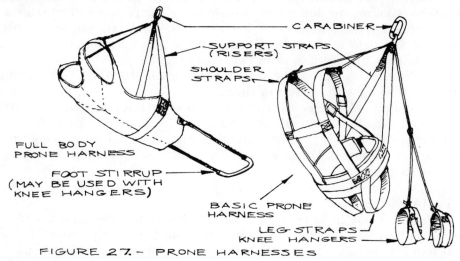

FIGURE 27. – PRONE HARNESSES

Flying with a seat harness is a treat. You sit in a good position to survey the countryside along the way. It feels natural since it's like driving a car. The drawbacks to the seated position are: greater drag, less control and the necessity to hold the glider higher on take off. It is the problems associated with take off that make seated flying less desireable for learning.

Figure 28 shows a seated and supine harness. Try to get these harnesses with individual leg straps – you'll find running on take-off to be much

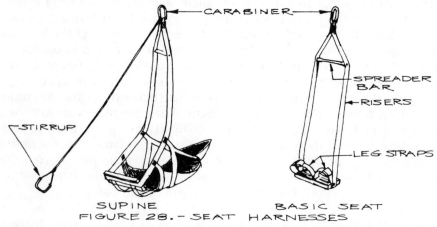

FIGURE 28. – SEAT HARNESSES

easier. As a beginner you'll not be concerned with flying supine. If you want to fly seated, locate a used seat harness – they are the cheapest set-up of all. A spreader bar should be in place in the risers. This keeps the straps from interfering with your head on take-off. You can make one

30

from wood as in figure 29. Make sure the attachment screws are flush with the straps so they do not catch. Inspect all straps carefully. The most likely place of damage is the strap that runs underneath the seat. Replace

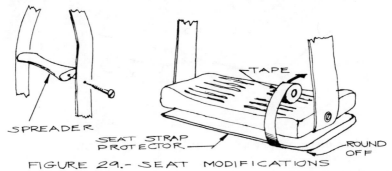

FIGURE 29.- SEAT MODIFICATIONS

it if it is frayed. You can protect it by adding padding or thin plywood and tape (see figure 29). This will also help you slide if you land on your seat. Be aware that some gliders are set up just for prone or just for seated. This has to do with the control bar placement. A "seated" glider should have the control bar set 2-4 inches (5-10 CM) forward of the perpendicular (see figure 30). The control bar positioning allows a comfortable arm

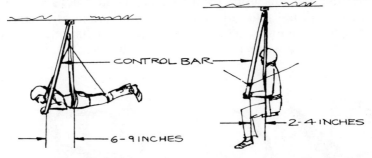

FIGURE 30. - CONTROL BAR ADJUSTMENT

placement and adequate room for control. Many modern gliders have provision for changing readily from seated to prone. Some of the methods include having different attachment points for the control bar on the lower front to back cables, adding short lengths of wire to these cables, having adjustments at the nose and tail of the keel to move the cables back and forth and turning the control bar around so that the back cables are in the front and vice versa. In the later case, the cables must have the proper relationship between them and the rear attachment point usually changes. One problem encountered is that increasing the tilt of the control bar actually decreases its vertical distance from the keel. This gives additional slack to the wires and allows more reflex. This is avoided by spacers at the nose and tail or at the control bar. Figure 31 shows one solution and demonstrates the proper position of the spacers (tangs).

At any rate, the seller of the glider may be able to tell you how the glider is set up (don't rely on him totally as pilots have been known to fly with their control bar positioned wrong). If the glider does not have the position you want and does not adjust you will have to have a qualified

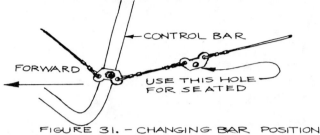

FIGURE 31. – CHANGING BAR POSITION

dealer (rigger) make a proper set of cables, or order them from the manufacturer.

Along with the harness you must consider the method of attachment to the glider. Most harnesses have a loop at the end of the support straps that accepts a carabiner. The carabiner then hooks on a rope tied to the glider or a bolt through the control bar. The rope is preferred as it has some elasticity which relieves stress during turbulence. The best ropes to use are braided polypropylene or synthetic mountain climbing rope. The polyprophylene should be fed inside itself to make a continuous loop as shown in figure 32. It will not pull out since the braid tightens as weight is applied. The mountain climbing rope can be tied as in figure 33. Any other form of knot tends to weaken the rope by as much as 50%. Use these con-

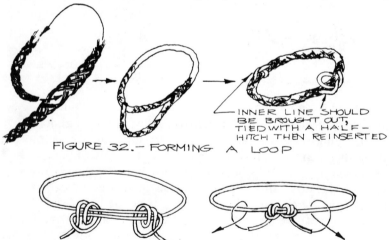

FIGURE 32. – FORMING A LOOP

FIGURE 33. – TYING FLEXIBLE ROPE

tinuous loops in the manner illustrated in figure 34. A second rope is advisable as a back up system as shown. This second rope should not hold any weight in normal operation. The ropes should be able to withstand 3000 lbs. This is much more than the glider could hold, but unattended wear greatly reduces the rope strength. Ropes are cheap, replace them when they wear.

An alternate method of hook-up is a quick release. These devises release the harness when a line is pulled. They will not release when weight is on the harness straps. A Quick release is a good safety measure when flying over trees or water. A no. 8 Maillon quick link will allow any harness to hook to a quick release.

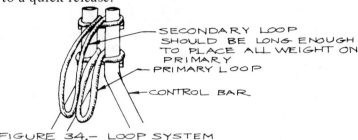

SECONDARY LOOP
SHOULD BE LONG ENOUGH
TO PLACE ALL WEIGHT ON
PRIMARY
PRIMARY LOOP

CONTROL BAR

FIGURE 34.— LOOP SYSTEM

THE HELMET

Years of experience have taught us that helmets are worth the hassle. Flying free and unfettered is certainly attractive, but human beings make errors and can't afford to gamble on hitting their head on a rock without protection. Respected, expert pilots wear helmets.

The helmet for you depends on how much you want to trade off price for protection. Usually, the more expensive models offer a better safety margin. Some manufacturers are offering special hang gliding helmets. The criteria for a good helmet is that it should provide adequate coverage of the head (rock climbing, Kayaking and bicycling helmets do not), have the ears open to hear the wind (to help judge airspeed) and be lightweight. Hardshell helmets are most often used, but the better models of hockey helmets may suit you. Make sure you get the proper size helmet so that the harness doesn't push it over your eyes on take off. Helmets are readily available from dealers or the hang gliding media.

MISCELLANEOUS EQUIPMENT

The most important and absolutely necessary piece of additional equipment for a beginner is a set of wheels. On every surface except sand, wheels will prevent the control bar from digging in and rotating the nose down to an abrupt stop. Without wheels you go sailing through the control bar on a nose-in. For a small investment wheels will protect you and the glider. If you are in a schooling situation, insist on using a glider with wheels.

There are several types of wheels available commercially. These, and a cheap, but durable, set you can make yourself are illustrated in figure 35. Put them on the control bar as shown with spacers and hose clamps (tape the clamps to prevent cuts). If your control bar is curved you will have to drill the center hole larger to slip around the curve and use a bushing to take up the extra space.

Gloves come in handy when learning on rough or rocky ground. Some loss of grip is often experienced with gloves. Knee pads are used by some schools for protection on hard surfaces. Wear long pants and tennis shoes. Boots are satisfactory, but there is a greater need for running ability than

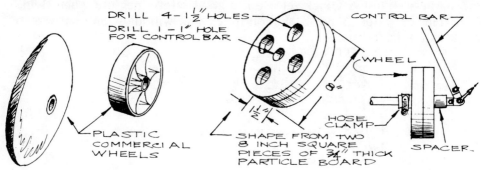

FIGURE 35. — WHEELS FOR BEGINNERS

for foot protection. All beginners should have rubber padding on the control bar. This helps if you ever bump into the bar and provides comfort to the neck and shoulders when carrying the glider. Refrigerator insulation hose is most suitable for this application. If you cut in about 2 ft. (.6 M) and leave it loose it can be pushed up out of the way on take-off and will fall down immediately afterward to pad the bar. The last bit of equipment you'll find useful is a wind meter. If you are flying with other pilots, chances are there will be a few around. If you want your own, contact a dealer or look in the hang gliding magazines. Wind meters are great for telling you when you shouldn't fly.

CARING FOR YOUR EQUIPMENT

Treat it well and it will free you from the earth; abuse it and it will let you down. You must take good care of your glider — your life depends on it. When transporting a glider on a car be sure to support it in as many places as possible. Unsupported ends can bounce violently and permanently bend tubes. You can use the control bar for support by tying it in the rear. If nothing else is available, use a short piece of tube, two rags and a rope as shown in figure 36. Get suggestions on racks from other pilots. There are many ingenious designs.

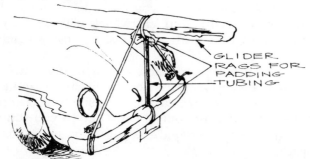

FIGURE 36. – TRANSPORTING THE GLIDER

When setting the folded gliders on racks or on the ground, do it gently to prevent bruising the sail and denting the tubes. The sail demands the most care. It is made from Dacron.® and impregnated with resin to reduce porosity. Everytime it is bent or wrinkled it looses resin. To help prevent this, lift the leading edges out — don't slide them on the sail. Roll the sail lightly when putting the glider away. Ties at different points will keep it in place. Do not leave the glider flapping in high winds. A glider should be tied or broken down in winds to prevent it from tumbling when left unattended. Try to park the glider in the shade as sunlight in combination with alkaline substances is the only thing that deteriorates Dacron®.

Cleaning a sail can be accomplished with soap and water. However, most soap is alkaline and must be rinsed 5 or 6 times or will damage the sail. Oil based stains can be successfully removed with mineral spirits. Try to remove grit and dirt with a light brushing followed by rinsing to avoid abrading the sail.

Maintaining the rest of the equipment is simple. Prevent it from undergoing hard knocks and rough handling. Do not allow the cables to kink and **never** step on them. A stone under a cable can fray it. Wind cables up in a neat roll when storing the glider and you'll have few problems. Protect the crossbar with tape or a piece of cloth if it contacts a bolt in the folded position.

The most obvious way to care for a glider is to use a good cover. All gliders should have covers. Transporting them without one damages the sail. Try to find a cover that opens lengthwise or splits in the middle. They are much easier to use and the glider doesn't have to lie on the ground during the setting up.

You should follow a regular maintenance schedule to keep your glider trouble free. The three areas of concern are the cables, spars and the sail.

1. Replace the cables once a year under heavy use. Near salt water you should replace them more frequently. Inspect your cables for rust between the strands frequently. If they are plastic coated, cut a small bit away and inspect for corrosion. The lower cables are the most critical.

2. Once every six months you should remove the sail and inspect the spars for dents or bends. Replace as necessary. Remove all bolts and nuts. Inspect for straightness and wear. Replace as necessary.

3. The sail should be inspected for severe cupping of the trailing edge. This is due to the hem stretching considerably less than the rest of the sail. Have a sailmaker correct this situation. Clean the sail every six months.

SUMMARY

From the preceding, the complexity of matching the equipment to the pilot can be appreciated. There are numerous designs and styles to choose from. Your best bet is to take your time and try to watch a number of gliders fly. Ask questions — most pilots are very helpful. Try to select a glider on the basis of performance, structural soundness, condition, style and price. It is advisable to choose one that is still being manufactured. Replacement parts aren't usually a problem, but changes in the sport may mean the design is outdated. If you still want that particular glider expect a price break.

Don't believe most manufacturer's performance claims. See for yourself how the glider behaves. Smart pilots will not buy a glider they haven't flown. If you can't yet fly, ask the opinion of as many pilots are you can. Remember that dealers have a vested interest in certain gliders. Don't buy a glider that has just come out on the market unless you know personally that the manufacturer has been refining it for at least six months. Invariably, the first few weeks of production bring out little problems. There have been gliders with design problems that don't appear until many are sold and months have passed. A proven design will not fail you unless you fail yourself in judgement and care.

CHAPTER IV

BEGINNING FLIGHT

Now it's time to try your wings. Learning to fly will probably be the most exciting thing you've ever done. Hang gliding is fun at all levels, so don't rush matters — master each step before moving to the next. Follow the program outlined in this chapter and you will be flying safely as soon as possible.

This beginning program is designed to follow the United States Hang Gliding Association Hang I program and incorporates the methods recommended for certified schools. Much emphasis is placed on running with the glider. To do this you must be in fair physical shape. One of the niceties of this sport is that you get exercise and have the best time of your life doing it. If you are not in shape you can still learn. Pace yourself and take frequent rests. Soon you'll be flying effortlessly.

SITE SELECTION

An inescapable requirement of hang gliding is a suitable hill. An ideal hill would be round to face in all directions, covered with grass, sloped from 15° to 30° and have plenty of run out room for landing. These hills are rare. If gliders are not already flying in your area, try to locate a slope that faces the prevailing (most common) wind. Often several sites are used to accomodate different winds. Figure 37 shows a good site with various glide paths imposed on it.

The slope angle must be greater than your glide angle. This is about 14° for a "standard" and less for all other designs. The slope should be clear of large rocks and stumps. A trip or a slide into one of these monsters is deadly. A path for running on take-off is necessary. Ruts or debris can reach out and grab a foot. A wide swath (at least four glider widths for beginners) should be clear of large trees.

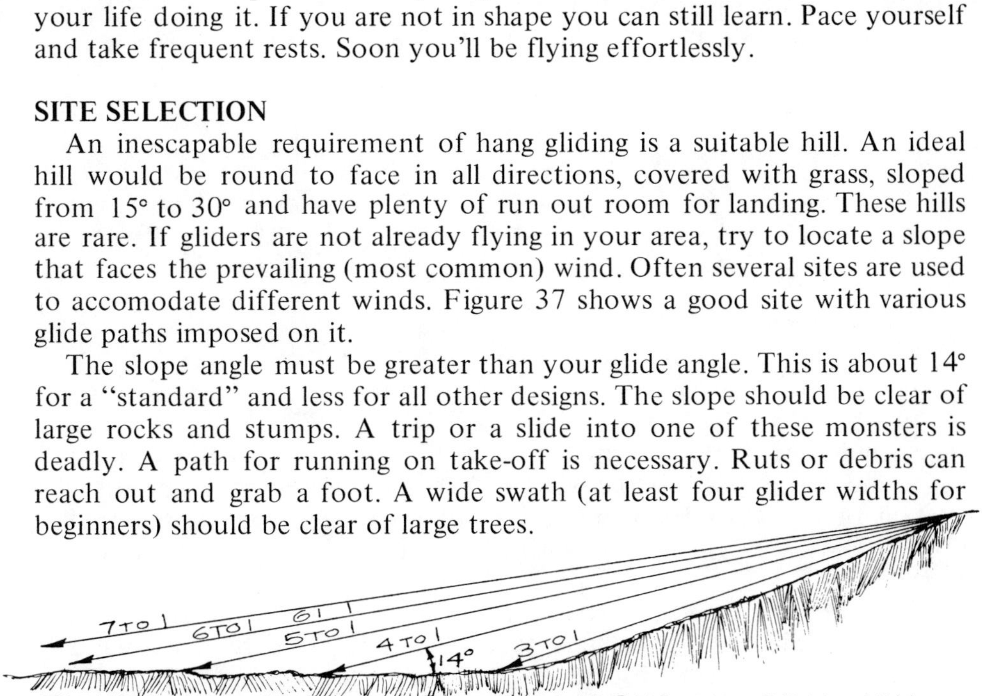

FIGURE 37. — GLIDE RATIO COMPARISONS ON IDEAL HILL

The landing area should be clear of buildings, ditches, trees and power lines. Also, keep the cars of spectators and your friends well away from the area. You will not be able to run an obstacle course when you first learn.

If you are flying on private property obtain the owner's permission. This can have varied results. Interestingly enough, rural folks are often glad to have you fly on their land. They invite their friends to see the bird-men. Pick up the trash and close the gates and everybody's happy. Land-owners who have experienced the realities of competitive society are a different story. They're afraid of being sued, and rightly so. However, they underestimate the safety of hang gliding today. It is your job to re-educate them. Become a member of the U.S.H.G.A. and you will auto-matically have liability insurance coverage. Prepare a professional sound-ing waiver form and have it ready when approaching a landowner. At all times be aware of his fears and show him you're a mature and responsible individual. Be mature and responsible by abiding by his wishes and taking care of his property. This means cleaning up after spectators and prevent-ing others from abusing his generosity.

WATCHING THE WIND

You must learn to see the wind. This takes imagination. Consider the wind to be like water flowing over and around solid objects in its path, swirling and rushing in a random fashion. There are three things you are trying to tell about the wind — its direction, velocity and degree of tur-bulence. You can tell direction from wind socks and streamers set up in strategic locations. Figure 38 illustrates these. In light winds, throw dried grass to tell direction. The wind must be directed up the hill for you to fly.

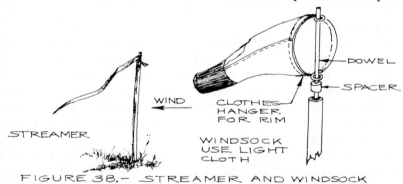

FIGURE 38.— STREAMER AND WINDSOCK

The wind velocity is indicated by a wind meter. Eventually you will learn to judge the speed of the wind by feel and observing the amount of flutter in the socks and streamers. Do not learn to fly in winds over 8 MPH (13 KMH) unless you are heavy for your glider. The ideal wind is 5-8 MPH.

Turbulence is a problem since it can exist with little indication of its presence. Turbulence is caused by solid objects in the path of the wind, or uneven surface heating. Figure 39 shows some situations where turbu-lence can be expected. The most common area of turbulence is downwind from a building or trees. Avoid these areas in any significant wind. Turbulence is most often felt as gusts or sudden changes in the wind velocity. These gusts throw the glider around in flight and require quick, deliberate control movements from the pilot. Needless to say, a beginner should not fly in turbulence. Build your experience up gradually. It is not fun to be caught in conditions you are not ready for. Learn to read these conditions.

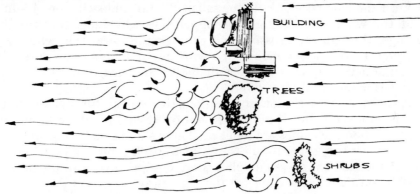

FIGURE 39. — TOP VIEW OF TURBULENCE

SETTING UP

Finally, all your preparations have paid off and you're at the site with your glider at your feet. The wind is perfect — gentle and straight up the hill. First you must set up. The following procedures outline the way almost all gliders set up. Follow them step by step and take care to do things correctly.

1. Orientate the glider so that the tail is to the wind. If you are setting the glider up alone, this is important (see step 8).

2. Open the cover and attach the control bar with the bolt or PIP pin provided. A PIP pin has a button that must be depressed to allow it to pass through the control bar bracket. If there are several choices of holes in the bracket, use the middle one or the one used by the previous owner. This positioning affects the trim (see Chapter VII). The control bar should be placed so that the bolts that hold it together are facing forward. This prevents cuts.

3. Attach the lower rigging (see figure 40). Be sure to have the control bar angled properly (for prone or seated) if there is an option.

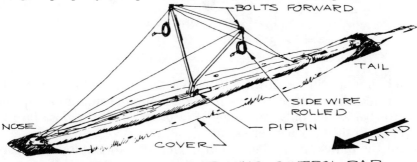

FIGURE 40. — ATTATCHING CONTROL BAR

39

4. Turn the glider over to stand on the control bar. Keep the tail on the ground.

5. Lift the kingpost and attach the free end of the front-to back cable (usually at the rear). Check again to see that nothing is twisted.

6. Swing the crossbar 90° to the rest of the spars. (see figure 41)

7. Unroll the side wires. Untie the sail at the tail and swing one leading edge. Put the wing bolt through the upper side wire tang, through the leading edge, through the crossbar and through the lower side wire tang. Finally fasten it with a locking nut or a wing nut and a pin (see figure 42). There is an added margin of safety if the bolt is inserted from the bottom up, but this is harder to do in a wind.

8. Repeat step 7 for the other side then tighten the turnbuckles until the slack is removed from all cables. Do not overtighten – there should be a low sound when the cables are plucked. There should be two turnbuckles – one at the rear (or front) for all the front-to-back cables and one on the side for all the side cables (some gliders are equipped with quick devises that attatch and tighten the cables at the same time).

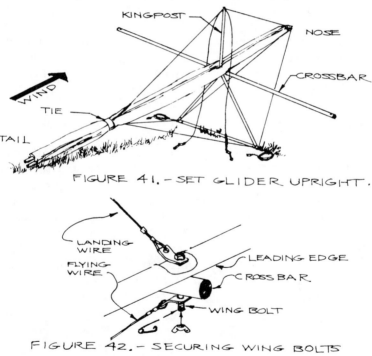

FIGURE 41. – SET GLIDER UPRIGHT.

FIGURE 42. – SECURING WING BOLTS

The tail should still be down and facing the wind. This prevents the glider from blowing over. Also this position limits the amount of bending on the crossbar when only one wing is in place. With the nose into the wind damage to the crossbar can occur.

9. Fold the deflexors in place (some gliders do not employ deflexors).

10. Grasp the nose of the glider and pull the tail slightly off the ground.

Swing the glider around quickly and put the nose down facing the wind. From this point on, the nose should always face into the wind (except during disassembly) and also be on the ground when the glider is not being used. During the early stages when you are using wheels, the glider may tend to roll with the wind. It helps to tie the wheels when at rest.

11. Insert the battens in the sail. Be sure they are properly hooked.

12. Preflight your glider. This is a walk-around inspection procedure necessarry for all aircraft. Learn to develop a set routine for inspection and over-look nothing. Here are some guildelines:

a. Start at the nose and inspect all bolts, nuts and cable attachments. To be safe, threads must protrude from all nuts. Sight down the tubes for alignment, straightness and reflex. Check the sail attachment.

b. Moving down one side, feel the leading edge for dents. Look at the wing bolt for flaws then sight the crossbar for straightness. Look at the sail attachment at the rear of the leading edge.

c. Move to the tail of the keel and inspect the cable ends. Inspect the sail attachment.

d. Move around the remaining leading edge and follow guideline (b).

e. Inspect the upper cables and make sure the kingpost is perpendicular.

f. Run your hands down the length of all the lower cables. This will detect any fraying or damage before it gets worse. Inspect the thimbles and shackles at the control bar.

g. Finally, ,check out the entire control bar, control bar bracket and heart bolt. Inspect your hook up system and harness thoroughly.

GROUND HANDLING

Now it's time to learn how to carry, balance and run with the glider. We begin without the harness on level ground. To carry a glider, turn backwards and crawl behind the control bar. Figure 43 illustrates the proper hand position. Use your shoulders and rotate the nose off the ground until

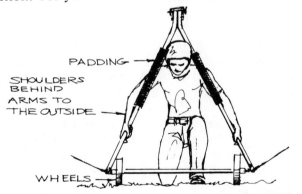

PADDING

SHOULDERS
BEHIND
ARMS TO
THE OUTSIDE

WHEELS

FIGURE 43. — LIFTING THE GLIDER

the keel is horizontal. Lift with your legs (not your back). This position allows you to walk forward (up a hill) with the nose still facing the wind. If you are walking towards the wind, turn your body around, not the glider. If you get the nose too low, the wind will push the glider down and strain your muscles. If the nose is raised too much the wind could blow the glider over. In the latter case, do not fight the glider — you are in no position to do so at the control bar. Let it blow over, then turn the glider on the kingpost so that the downwind leading edge is perpendicular to the wind direction. Let this leading edge fall to the ground and the glider will right itself. Holding on to a glider when it is blowing over often breaks a leading edge.

Situate yourself in an area with plenty of run-out room. Block the control bar with your foot and grasp the control bar near the top (the higher the better). Pull back and lift the nose until the keel is horizontal. Check the wind direction. Always keep a piece of yarn (known as a tell-tale) tied to a nose wire. Place the yarn about a foot down the wire to avoid interference from the sail. Turn the glider until the yarn is coming straight at you and lift it to the position shown in figure 44. Move the nose up and down slightly and find the balance point. This is very important. You should not have to use a lot of strength to keep the glider in position. Invariably, a beginner fails to balance the glider and has to use too much muscle power. Time and practice will bring success.

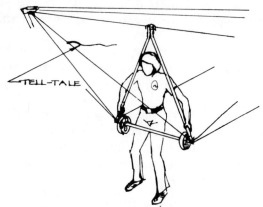

FIGURE 44. – HOLDING THE GLIDER

After you feel comfortable drop one hand (either will do) to the control bar horizontal. Place the other hand on the upright as in figure 45. This is the take-off position. The lower hand holds the control glider up and the upper hand controls the angle of the nose (pitch). While standing still, practice raising and lowering the nose by moving the upper hand forward and back. This will feel very awkward at first, but in the course of one day will become an automatic control. Set the glider down and rest. Think about the controls. Pulling the upper arm back lifts the nose so that the sail fills and the glider lifts. When actually taking-off this is a very small movement. Think about short, precise controls.

Do a few stretching exercises at this point. This will get your blood circulating, limber your muscles and relax you. Remember, the more relaxed you are, the quicker you will learn. Put on your helmet. Now lift the glider again and move the hands to take-off position once everything is in balance. Start to run gradually then pick up speed until you are

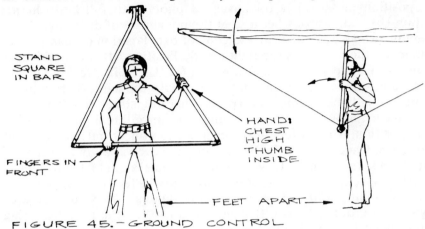

STAND
SQUARE
IN BAR

FINGERS IN
FRONT

HAND;
CHEST
HIGH
THUMB
INSIDE

————FEET APART————

FIGURE 45.—GROUND CONTROL

moving as fast as you care to. Pull the nose up and feel the glider lift. Keep running and drop the upper hand to the horizontal bar. The glider will not lift you at this point, so don't hang from it. Slow down gradully and put a hand back up to help ease it down. Repeat this until you are running at top speed and controlling the glider consistantly. You must keep the glider level until top speed is reached, then lift the nose slightly. If you start out too nose-high, the glider will act like a drag chute and you'll never get running speed. If you start out too nose low, the nose will drop abruptly and dig in the ground the moment you start running.

At this point you are ready to put on your harness and try the same thing with your body hooked to the glider. Be sure to wear a helmet and stay on level ground for now. With the basic prone harness you step through the leg straps and put the shoulder straps in position. The waist strap fastens at the back (usually with velcro). Have a friend help you straighten out the tangle of lines. Hook up to your glider and hang in flying position while a buddy holds the nose up (keel level). You should be lying on the bar or a little above it. Eventually, you will be two or more inches above the bar, but for now stay low so that you don't have to lie perfectly flat. The higher you are suspended, the quicker the pitch response. The final test of proper suspension length is lifting the glider and putting your hands in take-off position. You must hold the glider so that the suspension straps are tight throughout the entire take-off. Make sure the straps are adjusted so that you are comfortable holding the glider.

A seated harness stays with the glider. Simply lift the seat and strap it in position. Raise the glider and get a feel for the take-off position. Unfortunately when flying seated you are below the bar so that you must hold the glider higher on take-off. Try resting the control bar on your belt buckle. Remember to keep the straps tight and in front of your arms and

43

shoulders. This gives you an extra point of control when lifting the nose to take-off.

Alternate methods of holding the control bar are shown in figure 46. The position in 46 (a) is for advanced pilots with full body harnesses. Position (b) is dangerous because of the possibility of dislocated elbows if a nose-in swings you through the control bar. Position (c) can be used by beginners if the harness is the right length. Position (d) is a combination of the recommended position and position (c). Use it if it feels comfortable.

You are now ready to run on the level with the harness attatched. You can use your back against the (prone) harness straps to lift the nose to level the keel. Stoop down, lift the glider, balance it and put your hands in flying position. Take a few deep breaths and concentrate on keeping the glider level. Check to see that both wings are even and your harness straps tight. Check the wind with your tell-tale. Start a gradual run. When you reach top speed, ease the nose up and you will feel the glider try to lift you. Don't jump into it! It won't generate enough lift while you are running on flat ground. Notice that now you can lift the nose by easing the bottom hand forward if you keep the harness straps tight. If you let the glider sag you can still lift the nose by pulling back the upper hand.

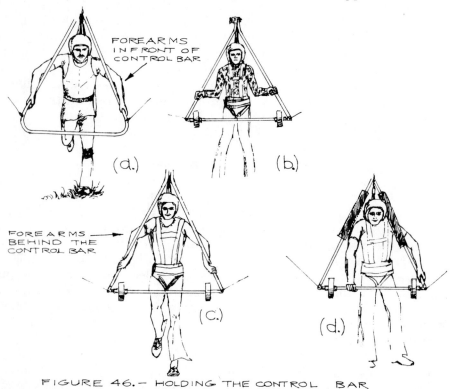

FOREARMS IN FRONT OF CONTROL BAR

(a.)

(b.)

FOREARMS BEHIND THE CONTROL BAR

(c.)

(d.)

FIGURE 46. — HOLDING THE CONTROL BAR

Now that you are hooked to the glider you must learn to do a proper stop. This will prepare you for landing. When you want to slow down and

44

stop, lean forward and push out on the bar. You may come off the ground slightly (if you have a proper energetic run) so bring your feet under you and stand up. Don't try to stop by slowing your body and the glider down with your legs. It just won't work. The nose of the glider will come down abruptly. Make the glider do all the work by pushing the control bar full forward. Do this successfully several times and you will be ready to move to the hill.

TAKING OFF

Here's what you've been waiting for. Take your time, relax and review what you have learned. Stand facing into the wind and close your eyes. Put your hands in take off position and imagine the feel of the glider. In your mind go through a complete take-off. Picture yourself running with the glider and do the proper control movements. You can learn to make the proper controls automatic this way because you can relax. When you are first learning, the adrenalin is flowing and your thinking may be somewhat unorganized.

Beware of fatigue. When your adrenalin level is high you are excited and you feel like you have plenty of energy. However, this is very taxing to your system and you will reach a fatigue point much sooner than otherwise. Take plenty of rests and don't take-off directly after carrying the glider up the hill.

Start a few feet up the slope. Prepare yourself and run the same as you did on the flat. Lean into your run and gently lift the nose when you reach top speed. If your feet lift off the ground, try to maintain airspeed by pulling the control bar in slightly (1 to 3 inches – 2 to 8 CM) then land gently by pushing full forward when your feet near the ground. Your first flights should only be a foot or two off the ground. Always land on your feet. Immediately after landing, set the glider down into the wind, drop the nose and unhook. Failure to do this could mean a broken glider if the wind blows it over with you attached.

If you are prone, keep your feet behind you at all times until landing. If you thrust your legs forward you change the center of gravity so that the glider wants to dive (see figure 47). If you feel that the glider is getting ahead of you, your only recourse is to run as fast as you can and dive into the bar pushing full out. Often this will effect a take-off. At worst, the glider will hit the ground and roll along on the wheels. Think about this emergency technique – it is the only way to prevent a hard nose-in.

If you are seated, keep your feet under your seat. Thrusting them forward again makes the glider tend to dive and leaves you vulnerable to tail bone injuries. Land on your feet! Wheels help reduce the severity of a nose-in when you are seated, but you can't ride the glider to a stop. Nose-ins are simply a result of starting out with the wrong nose angle, or letting it drop while running. Figure 48 illustrates this problem. When a beginner starts running he leans forward and often drops the nose as he does so. Also, his back interferes with the straps so that as soon as he leans into his run the harness is slack.

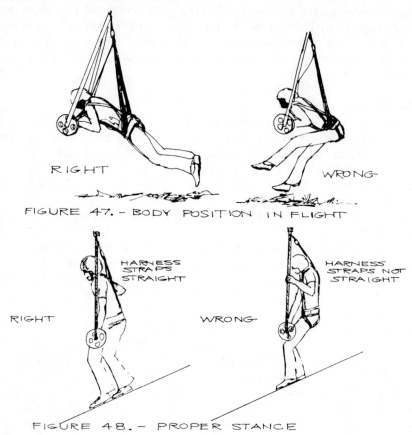

FIGURE 47. – BODY POSITION IN FLIGHT

FIGURE 48. – PROPER STANCE

Follow these steps for a good take-off:

1. Hold proper nose angle (level with the horizon). Too high and you will not get flying speed. Too low and you'll nose in.

2. Keep the wings level. If one wing is dropped you'll turn to that direction immediately.

3. Head directly into the wind. You will turn away from the wind otherwise.

4. Give a good strong run. This is the real secret to a good take-off. Imagine that you are running to the bottom of the hill.

5. Rotate nose upward. If your harness straps are tight this is simply a slight forward push.

6. Drop upper hand to the control bar horizontal. Your hands should be placed as in figure 49. This allows plenty of arm movement for quick lateral control.

Once you can do this successfully you are ready to move up the hill. Stay low until you are confident and your take-off is consistant. Then

46

move up in five foot steps. Eventually, you can move up ten, twenty and an even greater number of feet between flights, but first you must learn to control level flights and landings.

HANDS ON HORIZONTAL BAR

FIGURE 49. — FLYING POSITION

LEVEL FLIGHT

By now you've had the indescribable thrill of flying along a few feet off the ground. It's time to concentrate on controlling this flight. The first thing to note is the control direction and amount. Pushing forward on the bar (in flight) will raise the nose and slow you down. If you have excess speed you may rise a little. Pulling the bar toward you pulls the nose down so that you dive and speed up. If you are experienced at flying conventional aircraft, think of your body as the stick and push your body back or forward for nose up and nose down. The amount of pitch control needed in level flight is very minimal. Movements of as little as an inch have a noticeable effect. Practice without the glider, making quick deliberate control movements. Think: "slow down, speed up" as you do this.

You must learn to judge airspeed by the feel of the wind in your face and the sound of the air rushing by. Do not dive too fast or fly too slow. A fast dive makes turbulence worse and things happen too quickly. Flying too slow reduces control or stalls the glider. As a beginner you must learn to avoid a stall like the plague. A stall is simply caused by pushing out too far. If you feel everything is quiet then you are stalled. Pull in quickly (this is a much greater amount than normal control) to get the wing flying again if you are above 10 ft. (3 M) and the stall is not too great. Below this height it is wiser to try to keep the glider level and parachute down. The glider may tend to fall off on one wing and the leading edge may break. Obviously, a wise pilot will learn to avoid stalls before he is flying much higher than several feet. The solution is to relax and concentrate on airspeed. A glider that is in proper trim will fly at a proper airspeed with no input from the pilot. For this reason, level flight is extremely simple -- just don't fight the glider. Have an expert pilot check your glider for trim.

Do you notice how some flights seem to cover a lot of ground and others end very short? This has to do with the quality of your take off and how fast you fly. If you slow down too much you are creating lots

47

of drag and you don't go as far. If you speed up too much you loose altitude and again land short. Put a target spot in front of you and try to reach it. Vary your airspeed and see the difference. Hold your head out a car window at various speeds to get the feel of the wind force. You will want to start flying at 20-23 MPH (32-37 KPH).

LANDING

You must land into the wind. Therefore, fly into the wind at all times until you learn to turn. The object of a good landing is to reduce your ground speed to zero and set down gently on your feet. The wind affects your ground speed in the following manner: suppose you are flying at 18 MPH into an 8 MPH wind. Your groundspeed is 10 MPH (see figure 50). If you are flying with the wind your ground speed would be 8 + 18 = 26 MPH. A big difference. Landing into the wind minimizes your ground speed.

A proper landing is a precise coordination of speed and amount of push out, varied according to height and wind velocity. The best way to land is to maintain good airspeed until you are a few feet off the ground

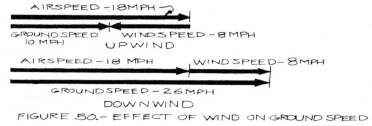

FIGURE 50.- EFFECT OF WIND ON GROUND SPEED

then push forward smoothly and rapidly. The slower you are flying, the faster this push out should be. The lower you are to the ground the faster should be the push. The higher the wind the less amount of push out you need. Be careful of getting the nose too high in a strong wind. If you are near the ground with too much speed wait till you slow down to push out or you will zoom up and be dangling helpless.

The act of pushing full out stalls the glider and stops you, at the same time dropping you to the ground. This braking action is called "flaring". Watch the birds land. They do a good job of flaring. The real key to a good landing is practice. You have to learn to sense the right time to pop the nose up. Concentrate on landing until you consistantly land at a stand-still on your feet.

There are two factors that complicate landings. The first is wind gradient and the second is ground effect. Wind gradient is a slowing of the wind as the ground is approached. This is caused by the drag created by the ground surface. Figure 51 shows how wind gradient can cause a stall. The pilot has plenty of airspeed at 20 ft., but enters into lower velocity winds without enough momentum to make him speed up above stall speed. Wind gradient varies according to wind velocity, surface texture and air stability (see Hang Gliding and Flying Conditions). To

48

overcome the wind gradient problem, simply speed up as you approach the ground.

A particularly dangerous form of wind gradient is called wind shadow. This is a calm area downwind from a building, row of trees or similar

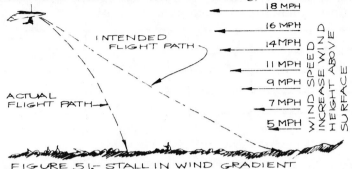

FIGURE 51.- STALL IN WIND GRADIENT

obstruction. The problems wind shadow creates are bad stalls, since it represents an extreme gradient. If you must land in a protected area when there is a wind, approach the landing so that you go through the gradient level across the wind. There will then be no difference felt by the glider.

Ground effect is an apparent cushioning of the air as you approach the ground. This is due to the reduction of wing tip vorticies (see Chapter VI). On your first few flights you probably won't even notice it since you will always be flying in ground effect. The result of ground effect is to make the glider go a lot further than it normally would. This means you must allow yourself extra run-out space. If you are nosing in on the landing (a common occurance with inexperienced pilots on higher performing gliders) then you are flying too slow. The ground effect gives you a good glide ratio at slow speeds, but you don't have enough moving kinetic energy to flare properly.

THE END OF THE DAY

After a happy day of learning to fly your responsibilities to yourself are not over. Of course, you must put your glider away. To do this, follow the procedures for set-up in reverse order. Be sure to coil any loose cables to keep them undamaged. Roll the battens in the sail. Tie the leading edges to the keel after the wings and sail are folded. Store the glider on a dry, safe rack. Lock it if you can — there have been cases of stolen wings.

An additional necessity is to fill out a log book. The reason for this is to keep a record of progress for review of site directors and give you a source of information when looking for problems. A log book can be just a notebook or you can purchase one made specially for hang gliding. An example of a log book appears in figure 52. If you get an instructor to sign your accomplishments and you have progressed to this point you should have earned your Hang I rating and be well on the way to Hang II.

Continue practicing take offs and landing until you are flying level with about 15-20 ft. (4.5-6 M) ground clearnace. You will then be ready to start turns (Chapter V). In the mean time, learn to use your knee hangers and raise your harness to lie flat (if you'fly prone). Keep your wheels on until you have attained a stable take off.

DATE	FLIGHT DESCRIPTION	LOCATION	CONDITIONS	GLIDER	WITNESS
7/77 MARCH	SOARED FOR 1 HR. IN MILD LIFT. 5 360's 1200 FT VERTICAL	MAGIC MT., KANSAS	WINDS 8-12 SMOOTH, WARM	SKY KING	*Otto Lilienthal*

FIGURE 52.— LOG BOOK EXAMPLE

SUMMARY

You have learned to fly! At night while lying in bed review your learning. Go through entire flights in your mind. You have mastered the hardest part. The rest is easy. If you experienced fear do not worry. This is a natural reaction. Overcome it by staying at one level until you have the confidence to move on. Watch the birds. A fledgling has as much trouble as you, learning to fly. Try to think flying all the time (it's hard to avoid). Watch the hawks soar and the clouds sail on the wind. You will soon join them.

The hardest part to learn is the take-off. The secret is learning to balance the glider, keep it level, then run while maintaining the balance. A higher performance glider will do practically all the work for you since it is stable in pitch if you run fast enough.

The following set of rules should be memorized and practiced always for the sake of safety.

1. Never fly alone.

2. Never fly when tired.

3. Never fly under the influence of alcohol or drugs.

4. Always take off and land into the wind.

5. Keep the nose down and unhook when the flight ends.

6. Follow these take-off procedures:

   a. Preflight the glider.

   b. Clear landing area and check wind.

   c. Hook-up

   d. Check wind at take-off.

   e. Recheck hook-up.

   f. Lift glider and set nose attitude.

   g. Run!

50

CHAPTER V

INTERMEDIATE FLIGHT

By now you have become familiar with your glider and flying controls. The next step is to increase your skills to enable you to handle varying conditions and situations. It has been said that wind is a complicating factor in any type of flying. This is especially true for hang gliding. You must learn to use the wind to your benefit.

Flying in strong winds at higher altitudes requires the ability to maneuver and control the glider's direction. Learning to turn is the secret to being in total command of your aircraft and ultimately being totally free in the air.

FLYING IN WIND

The force of the wind increases as the square of the velocity. This means that if the wind speed is doubled, the force goes up four times. This force is what acts on your glider and tries to control you if you don't control it. You must learn this control gradually. By the time you have aquired all the knowledge and skills in this chapter you may be flying winds up to 15 MPH (24 KPH), but this ability comes after months of carefully working with slight increases in wind velocity. One of the reasons it takes months is that you cannot control the winds. Don't get impatient. Wait for the right conditions. By now you should be aware that the wind is usually stronger higher up the hill. Use this phenomena to choose the wind velocity you can handle.

The problems associated with winds are turbulence and controlling ground path. Turbulence was mentioned before with a warning to avoid it. You can, however, fly safely in turbulence if you learn to make the proper corrections at the proper time. These consist of moving forward or back, left or right on the control bar to correct for pitching, rolling or yawing of the glider. We will learn more of this in a later section.

Flying in turbulence is a matter of degrees. There is some point where the pilot's ability will not serve to maintain control. Since turbulence is associated with higher winds, fly in lower velocities as you develop your skill. The speed you fly at greatly affects your ability to handle turbulence. If you fly too slow you have less control (the glider reacts slower) and a gust can put you in a stall. If you fly too fast you actually increase the strength and effect of the turbulence. The best speed to fly is close to the glider's maximum glide ratio speed (this is covered in Chapter II).

Controlling your ground path in winds is a matter of making calculations in your mind, reviewing the situation, recalculating, correcting control and so forth, all automatically. The problem is parallel to that of a boat in a river. The stronger the current, the slower the going is upstream while the downstream velocity is great. You are flying the air at all times just like the boat captain maneuvers in the water. However, when you are below 100 FT. (30 M) you must be concerned about your velocity in relationship to the ground. At all times your velocity in the air will be added to the wind velocity to determine your velocity over the ground. For instance, if you are flying 20 MPH in a 15 MPH headwind you will only be moving over the ground at 5 MPH.

The complication comes when you are flying in a cross wind. In figure 53 (a) we see a pilot trying to go from point X to point Y. The wind is 15 MPH from his right. If he is flying at 20 MPH and heading directly at point Y he will find that he ends up at Z. The wind velocity has added to his flying velocity and given him a ground path very different from the one he intended. To get to point Y, the pilot must angle his heading partially upwind (53 (b) so that a portion of his flying velocity exactly compensates for the wind velocity. This is called "crabbing into the wind" because the glider moves sideways like a crab scuttling across a beach.

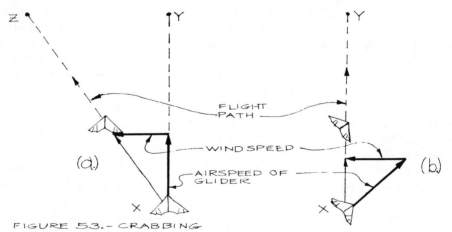

FIGURE 53.- CRABBING

The amount of "crab angle" necessary depends on your flying velocity, the velocity of the wind and the direction you wish to go with respect to the wind. The wind does not control where you go. It does, however determine what heading you must take to get there.

Wind will change your effective glide ratio over the ground. Think about it this: If your best glide ratio comes at a speed of 23 MPH and you are flying into a 23 MPH headwind you will be going nowhere — even at your best glide ratio. However, if you speed up you will begin to make some headway. Thus,we can see that speed to fly for best glide ratio over the ground is different than the speed to fly for best glide relative to the air. Figure 54 demonstrates the change in glide path with a change in wind, sink or lift. All these matters must be considered when flying in winds. Learn to develop these skills gradually so they become automatic before they become necessary in an emergency situation.

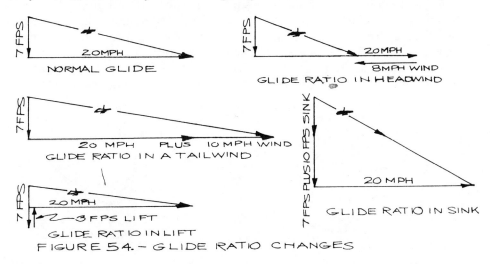

FIGURE 54. — GLIDE RATIO CHANGES

TURNS

With an understanding of the effect of wind, we can use turns to optimize our flight path. First however, we must learn to coordinate turns in nearly calm conditions. In Chapter II we learned that a turn is initiated by moving to one side of the control bar, thus rolling the glider. Start out doing turns by doing just that.

From a point on the hill that provides you with about 20 FT. (6 M) of altitude over a large, clear area, take off and fly level. When you get your maximum altitude, check your speed (you should be going about your best glide) then push your body slightly to one side of the bar. A wing will dip and the glider will turn gently. Try this in both directions. The turns should only be a few degrees. The next step is to get a little more height and try a greater turning angle. This time, speed up slightly just before you bank to one side. Then, as soon as the glider reacts by rolling, push forward a slight amount. Notice the difference? A true co-ordinated turn is a unique combination of entry speed, bank angle and push out. The faster you enter the turn the more you can bank and push forward. Without the forward push, the glider will not want to turn, but will sideslip. You will loose a lot of altitude in your turn if you fail to push out adequately. Pushing out too much results in a stall, just like in straight ahead flight. However, there are complications to a stall in a turn. For one thing, the inside wing is moving much slower than the outside

53

wing. Thus, this wing stalls first and drops dramatically. What usually happens at this point is the glider spins unless the pilot is quick to pull in the control bar and get the inside wing flying again. Avoid stalls in a turn by learning the controls gradually, in shallow turns.

To stop a turn, you reverse the control action. That is, you begin pulling in and move to the outside of the turn to start the roll out. Once you are level, correct your speed. Figure 55 illustrates a turn from start to finish. In 55 (a) the pilot gets sufficient speed then banks to the left. He will sense a slight falling to this side. In the same motion, he begins to push the bar forward. This starts the glider turning (b). The turning action creates a centrifugal force which centers his body (c). The pilot will feel heavier because of the centrifugal force, and he will feel the bar pushing back at him stronger than usual. At (d) he rolls the glider back to level.

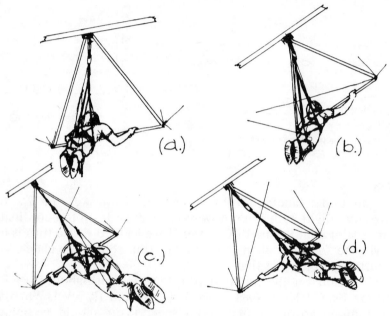

FIGURE 55.—TURN CONTROLS

A common mistake that beginners make when learning to turn is turning their body. The proper control movement is moving the entire body to one side, not twisting (see figure 56). There are several exercises to help you learn this. One method is to hold the hands in flying position (without the glider) and run along moving to the left or right as you move your hands to the right or left. This will teach you automatic response, so necessary when flying in turbulence. Another method is grasping a steering column in the manner you hold a control bar. A turn with the vehicle will then be performed the same as with the glider — with push out and all! Practice doing turns at different speeds, with different bank angles. Start with gentle turns then progress to turns of up to 90°. A perfectly co-ordinated turn could be continued forever if space allowed. The mark of a good pilot is his mastery of turns.

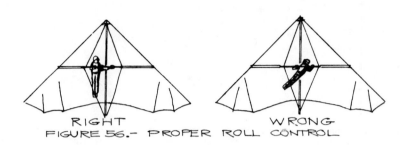

RIGHT   WRONG
FIGURE 56.— PROPER ROLL CONTROL

Once you have learned to turn in one direction in fairly light winds, you should combine turns to the left and right so that you can end up still heading into the wind. These are called S turns. Eventually you want to perform linked 90's. These are consecutive 90° turns in different directions. These maneuvers allow you to practice turns in higher winds. Do not turn more than perpendicular to the wind until you have accomplished many safe controlled turns.

Eventually, you will work your way up to 180° turns. Your first 180° turns should be accomplished in light winds. Start with a 90° turn so you are heading across the wind. Do a 180 to head back the other way, then finish with a 90 to land into the wind. After perfecting this in both directions, progress to back-to-back 180's. Perfecting these manuevers will give you all the expertise needed to fly almost any site.

The danger of turning in wind is one of misjudgement. When you turn into the wind your ground speed is slowed. When you turn away from the wind you are accelerated suddenly to a much higher ground speed. An inexperienced pilot may think that he is diving and push out, only to stall. A downwind stall is disasterous since there is no control and you are moving with the wind into the hill. All you can do is dive quickly and hope you can turn before you hit the hill. Do not attempt a turn away from the wind until you are much more advanced.

Another problem when turning in wind close to the ground is a result of the wind gradient. In figure 57 we see that the upper wing will be in higher velocity winds. Thus, when turning upwind it will feel like something is fighting you. When turning downwind you will tend to over-roll in a steep bank. Don't turn downwind close to the ground even when you are experienced. There's no room for error.

The most efficient turn is the one that loses the least amount of altitude. If you turn slow and flat you minimize the increase in sink rate, but the turn takes too long and you lose anyway. If you turn very steep you complete the turn very quickly but have a great sink rate. The most efficient turn is midway between the two extremes. This is a turn with a 45° angle of bank. In thermals (see Chapter VII) the situation is somewhat different. The idea is to stay in the lift so that constant turning is necessary. Therefore there is no premium to completing the turn as quickly as

FIGURE 57. — TURNS IN WIND GRADIENT

possible. There is a need to remain close to the core of the thermal. Consequently bank angles from 20° to 30° prove most efficient. The latter bank angle applies to smaller, stronger thermals.

FLYING HIGHER

As you learn to turn you will need more height to make greater turns. Conversely, the better you can turn, the more able you will be to use up your altitude and maneuver to a landing area. Every flight should be preplanned. This means having a set flight path in mind and sticking to it. Know where you're going to cross a fence, which side of a tree you're going to pass, where you're going to enter the landing area etc. As you gain ability you can have a more general flight plan that gets more specific as you approach the landing area. It is wise to have alternate courses of action in the event of a suprise (the wind is known for its fickle nature).

As you fly higher you will probably experience what is known as the dive syndrome. On a pilot's first high flight he is so far away from the ground that nothing appears to be moving. "I'm flying too slow" he thinks and speeds up. Things aren't much better, so he dives some more. This state of affairs usually ends when he hears his sail flapping loudly or he nears the ground and sees he is setting speed records. Once on the ground he is pleased at having flown so high, but he kicks himself for having gone so fast. Avoid this problem by flying the air NOT the ground. Above a few hundred feet you must get all your speed reference from the feel of the wind. This means all the senses other than sight and smell.

As you fly higher you will have time to relax, survey the scenery and think about what you are doing. Make your control movements neat, keep your flying posture trim and carve your turns gracefully. Now is the time to get a good feel for your maximum L/D, minimum sink and stall speed. With several hundred feet of altitude, slow your glider down gradually. You should feel the controls begin to get sluggish. Push out a tiny bit more and you will feel it wallow and fight you. You may feel buffeting as the air turbulates over the upper surface. This is your stall point. Pull in immediately to regain flying speed. Notice how much altitude you lost. Now slow down to just above the stall speed. See if you can maintain this speed until you have to set up the landing. This is your minimum sink speed. At this flying speed you will remain in the air as long as possible. Your best L/D speed is found on a hill that allows you to fly straight out. Fly at different speeds until you find the one that takes you the farthest. It is very important to have a good feel for your glider in this manner. Some day you may need all the distance you can get to reach a landing area. An airspeed indicator will give you precise readings at the critical speeds so you can always maximize your performance.

LANDINGS

This is one of the most important topics in hang gliding. Every flight must end in a landing. The air doesn't hurt you, the ground does. The most important part of a landing is setting it up. This means being in the right place at the right time. Figure 58 shows a glider at a given altitude and the options for landing. If there is no area within the circle he is in trouble. To avoid this sort of trouble, always have the landing portion of

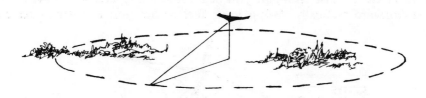

FIGURE 58. – LANDING OPTIONS

your flight plan well laid out. One way to do this is to imagine windows in the sky. The closer you are to landing the smaller the windows get. Progress from one window to the next, making continuous corrections. This prevents the problem of indecision and waiting until it's too late. The tried and true method of landing that aircraft utilize is that shown in figure 59. This consists of a downwind approach, a crosswind base and a final leg into the wind. This offers a lot of options. The approach and base legs can be lengthened and the turns at A and B can be slipped to lose more altitude. An intermediate pilot can learn this in very light winds, but should use an approach consisting of passes back and forth downwind of the target to loose altitude in any significant wind.

Learning to set up a landing is of course of utmost importance when spot landing. In fact, the best thing you can do from the moment you learn to fly is set out a spot and try to land directly upon it. Don't keep it in the same place. Your glider cover works well for this.

There may come a time when you have to land in adverse conditions. If you are landing in turbulence, approach the ground with moderate speed

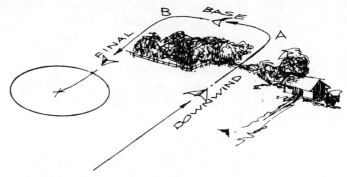

FIGURE 59.—LANDING APPROACH

and get very low before you flare. You may even have to drag the ground to stop without flaring too much and risking getting blown over. A cross-wind landing can be accomplished by dropping the upwind wing while flaring. This is almost the same as a turn. You want to prevent this wing from being lifted and flipping you (see figure 60). A downwind landing has one criteria — run. Keep the glider fairly fast and approach low to the ground. At the precise moment you begin losing airspeed you must throw the bar forward radically. Bring your feet under you and start running.

FIGURE 60.— CROSS WIND LANDING

If you do this properly you will only have to equal the wind speed.

Emergency landings are another problem. Flying in some locations means flying over trees. Given the tendency for humans to miscalculate, this means tree landings. Tree landings can be dangerous. The best way to land in a tree is to treat it as if it were a spot and land squarely in the middle. The biggest danger in a tree landing comes from hitting the tree and falling out. You slice through the air like a plate and crash to the ground if a wing is tilted upwards by the branches. When you land in a tree start grabbing. Get yourself hooked to a limb, detach from your glider and let it fend for itself. Your body is more valuable. If you are heading at a tree low and can't possibly land on it. throw the nose up vigorously just as your reach it and grasp anything you can. Think of your body only. A quick release comes in handy since carabiners are impossible to unhook if there is any weight on them.

58

Once you are safe and the adrenalin has subsided, you must rescue your glider. The only way is with a saw and rope. The tiniest branches hook the wires and hold the glider fast. Tie the rope to a solid part of the glider then loop it over a branch above. Cut off branches entangling the glider and lower it down (gently) as you progress. Learn from the experience and don't let it happen again.

Avoid power lines like you would a rabid dog. You have a right to fear them. The glider cables are very efficient at cutting insulation. There is no need to hit a power line. The problem comes from misjudged turns or simply not seeing them. Know your landing area well. Power lines are easy to see against the sky, but from the air may blend in with the ground. Look for poles and swaths cut through vegetation. Do everything possible including slipping to the ground to avoid a power line.

Emergency landings in a small field will be as successful as the pilot's state of preparedness. If you practice setting up landings, hitting spots, slipping turns to control altitude and parachuting the glider, you have the best chance possible of landing safely. A better form of preparedness is to plan flights carefully and have plenty of options if the plan is altered by unseen circumstances.

SUMMARY

In this chapter we learned more about the glider and the controls. Total maneuverability is possible in a hang glider with the proper practice and development of skills. Turns are fun. Swooping back and forth through the air has no parallel in earthbound pastimes.

The other half of good flying is being able to judge the conditions. The biggest problem is presented by high winds and turbulence. Learn to "see" gusts by watching the trees move at different intervals. You can watch a gust approaching through the grass or trees. It swirls violently as it comes. When it reaches you a blast is felt then it subsides to be replaced by another. Learn to observe the clouds to tell what kind of turbulence to expect. A day with puffy clouds or clear and sunny will be more turbulent.

At this point you are able to perform all the Hang II tasks and some of the Hang III tasks. Keep up the progress toward perfection in flight. The ultimate goal is to be one with the air. Be able to sense it and feel it. Learn to relax and sail through the sky like a great bird.

CHAPTER VI

ADVANCED AERODYNAMICS AND GLIDER DESIGN

In this chapter we take a closer look at the factors that make a glider safer and fly better. We will find that these two design criteria do not necessarily go hand-in-hand. Sometimes performance is limited by the need to maintain ample safety margins. Indeed, when it comes to performance alone, the designer is often required to find a happy median between glide ratio, sink rate, handling, convenience and portability. It is impossible to maximize all these qualities simultaneously. Consequently we have many types and styles of hang gliders suited to a wide variety of conditions and personal tastes.

An in-depth understanding of aerodynamics will help the student decide which glider he should own as well as augment his flying skill and awareness of safety requirements. Of course, the study of aerodynamics is a lifetime endeavor in itself, so we must be content with reviewing the highlights and concepts relating specifically to hang gliding. An active pilot will encounter many terms and technical references in conversations with other pilots. This will leave him quite bewildered unless some attempt is made to learn "What makes it fly".

STRUCTURAL STRENGTH

It is an obvious requirement for a glider to withstand the loads it encounters. What are these loads? Let's look at a standard glider with a 90° nose, 18 FT (6 M) spars and a 150 LB. (68.2 K) pilot. In steady flight, the tension and compression forces will appear as in figure 61. Without a doubt, the crossbar is under the greatest compression. However, the leading edge is the most vulnerable due to its unsupported free end. Higher performance gliders utilize shorter keels and longer leading edges. This changes the relationship of the forces so that the side wires experience a greater load while the fore and aft wires are under less tension. The leading edges need deflexors for support. A heavier pilot would increase the forces proportionatly for the same size glider.

We have been speaking of one "G" loads. This means the glider is lifting only the weight of the pilot due to the force of gravity. However, much greater G loads can be experienced when encountering vertical gusts or performing maneuvers. A gust is a swirling mass of air. When a glider encounters a gust, a bump is felt and the angle of attack changes.

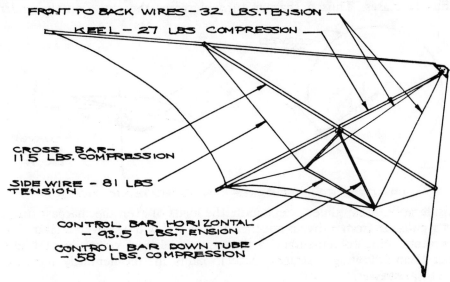

FRONT TO BACK WIRES – 32 LBS.TENSION

KEEL – 27 LBS COMPRESSION

CROSS BAR– 115 LBS. COMPRESSION

SIDE WIRE – 81 LBS TENSION

CONTROL BAR HORIZONTAL – 93.5 LBS.TENSION

CONTROL BAR DOWN TUBE – 58 LBS. COMPRESSION

FIGURE 61. — GLIDER FORCES

This change is due to the fact that the air in the gust is moving in a different direction from the normal air. You will recall from Chapter II that there is a unique angle of attack associated with each airspeed, regardless of the direction of air movement. This is only true if directional changes in the air are slow enough so that the glider can adjust airspeed to any new angle of attack presented. In a gust, a wing can suddenly acquire a high angle of attack while glider momentum maintains a high speed. This combination results in the sudden creation of a large lift force, upward acceleration, and consequently, increased structural loading. The following equation can be used to determine the amount of gust loading possible at a given speed.

$$\left(\frac{\text{Flying speed}}{\text{Stall speed}}\right)^2 = \text{G Loading}$$

From this relation, we can see that a glider flying at twice the stall speed can experience 4 times the normal load in a gust. The safe thing to do is fly slower in turbulent conditions.

The G loading increases in maneuvers due to centrifugal force. This can be illustrated by attaching a ball to a piece of string. Hold the free end of the string and swing the ball in a circle. Notice that the faster the ball is swung, the greater the force is on the string. The well known equation relating to circular motion is $F = mv^2/r$.

m = mass of the ball (or any weight moving in a curved path)

v = velocity of the weight

r = radius of the curved path.

We can relate the motion of the ball to a hang glider as in figure 62. From

61

the equation we can see that the force or G load increases as the mass (pilot weight) and velocity (flying speed) increases, but decreases as the radius increases. Thus a sharper turn increases the stress on the glider

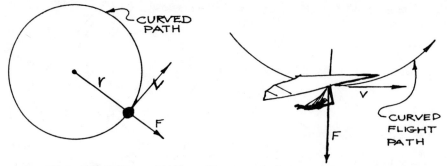

FIGURE 62. – FORCES IN CIRCULAR MOTION

considerably. Most gliders can handle the loads of even the sharpest turns, but a pull-out from a dive is another matter and will be covered later. The important thing to remember is that any condition, or mode of flight, other than following a straight path in calm air, momentarily increases structural stresses.

TURNS

The action of centrifugal force is one of the factors behind a hang glider's ability to turn. Recall from Chapter V that a co-ordinated turn requires a proper entry speed, a corresponding roll to the side and finally, a push out on the control bar. Let's take a look at the forces involved. In figure 63 (a) the pilot is flying straight ahead and his weight is balanced by the total upward forces on the glider (R). The pilot then shifts his weight to bank the glider to the left an amount indicated by θ in figure 63 (b). Note that R is no longer directed upwards so that the total up-ward forces R_1 are not equal to the weight. At this point one of two things (or a combinatin of both) will happen. The glider will either speed up and slip to the inside of the turn, or the pilot will push the control bar forward, increasing angle of attack. In the latter case, the vertical lift force R_1, will increase to equal the weight W (figure 63 c). At this point there is an unbalanced force R_2 which turns the glider to the left. As soon as the turn begins, centrifugal force swings the pilot's body to the right until it is centered (see figure 63 (d). Note that if the pilot holds himself on the left side of the bar as in 63 (b or c), he will not produce a coordinated turn, but will side-slip.

A slip is a falling towards the inside of a turn. This is pictured in figure 64. A slip can be dangerous due to the high velocities attainable. A glider can fall earthward much faster by slipping than when in a straight ahead dive. It is entirely possible to build up speed in a slip to the point that the forces created during pull-out are great enough to destroy the glider. An experienced pilot can use slipping turns very effectively to lose altitude rapidly when landing in small areas.

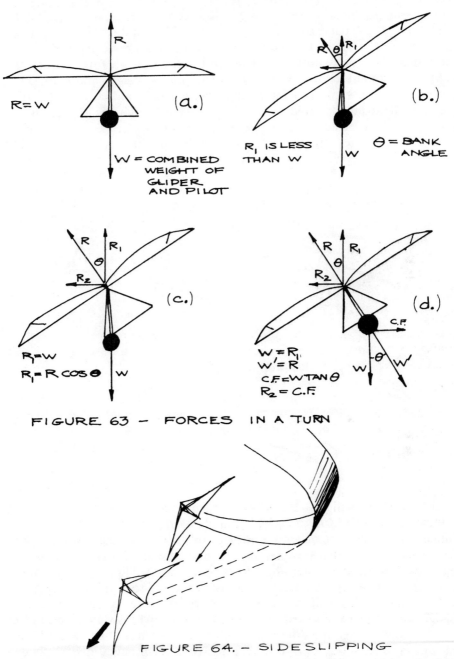

R

R = W

(a.)

W = COMBINED
WEIGHT OF
GLIDER
AND PILOT

R θ R₁

(b.)

R₁ IS LESS
THAN W

W

θ = BANK
ANGLE

R R₁
θ
R₂

(c.)

R=W
$R_1 = R \cos \theta$ W

R R₁
θ
R₂

(d.)

C.F.

W=R₁
W'=R
C.F.=W TAN θ
R₂ = C.F.

θ W'
W

FIGURE 63 — FORCES IN A TURN

FIGURE 64. — SIDESLIPPING

A glider with dihedral will tend to pull out of a slip by raising the lower wing. The forces causing this reaction are pictured in figure 64(a). If a glider is slipping to the left with the velocity S, the left wing will have a greater angle of attack. This will create a greater lift component and thus restore the glider to a level position.

Other sources of slip control are a low center of gravity, vertical fin surfaces and sweepback of the wings. Figure 65(b) indicates how a center of gravity located below the wing surface will cause a restoring force if the pilot remains in the center of the control bar. Since no turn is initiated, the lift component is not aligned with the pilot's weight and centrifugal force does not enter in as a factor maintaining the bank angle. The force on a vertical surface located above the center of gravity is also shown in figure 65(b). The effect of sweepback can be viewed in figure 65(c). Here the left wing is meeting the relative wind more directly than the right wing. This again creates a greater lift component and a restoring force.

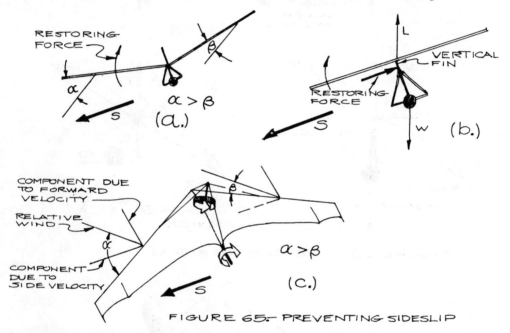

FIGURE 65.- PREVENTING SIDESLIP

In addition, there will be a tendency to turn to the left since the left wing developes more drag (due to its higher angle of attack).

Since a slip does not occur without a roll, and stopping a slip consists of rolling the wings back to level or equalizing the lift along the entire wing, it follows that the design factors that prevent slipping also make a glider hard to roll. Thus, a designer must trade off roll stability for quick roll response. Quick roll response is desireable when trying to stay in thermals and maneuver in patchy lift. The most obvious way to get better roll response is to reduce dihedral. Reducing the amount of sweep is also used, but is only about one sixth as effective as changing dihedral. Sweep is necessary for yaw stability and pitch damping, so has a limited range of variation in a given design.

In a flexible wing the initiation of a roll is followed by a brief shift in the sail towards the inside (lower) wing. This greatly aids the roll control. By adding a keel pocket, this sail shift is enhanced and quicker roll results. Another method of improving roll (and hence turning response) is adding aerodynamic controls — ailerons, elevons and dragelons. These devices are movable surfaces, at the wing tips controlled by the pilot. Their method of operation is to change the lift or drag (or both) on the wing so that the wing tilts or rolls (see figure 66). The use of these devices can eliminate the need for weight shift when turning and allows the designer much more latitude to vary other factors. The drawbacks of aerodynamic controls is

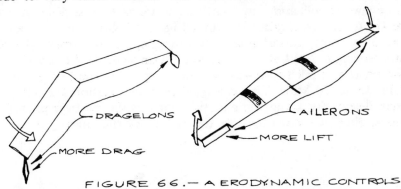

FIGURE 66. — AERODYNAMIC CONTROLS

their greater complexity and weight. It should be apparent that reducing the span (width) and tip weight of the glider will also promote better roll characteristics. This can be understood by noting that it is easier to swing a shorter, lighter baseball bat than a long, heavy one. In a later section, we will see that a wider span is desireable, so that ultimately aerodynamic controls may be necessary.

Yawing is a turning about a vertical axis. This occurs due to gusts, pilot body movement and differential drag. When a vertical gust hits a wing, the angle of attack, and hence, the drag is increased. This will make the wing fall back and yaw the glider. This yawing action is most pronounced in high performance gliders and is beneficial since it helps relieve the loading caused by the gust. A pilot can yaw a glider by swinging his body about a vertical axis. This is shown in figure 56. The prone flying position produces this effect more readily since the moment of inertia about the vertical axis of a prone pilot is one third that of the glider while a seated pilot's moment of inertia is about one tenth the glider's. Note that this action must be combined with a roll or no turn results. Differential drag is caused by the use of ailerons and results in adverse yaw. The glider in figure 66 using ailerons to effect a right turn is changing the average angle of attack of the wing tips. The left wing tip has an increased angle of attack, while the right wing has a decreased angle of attack. Consequently the left wing will rise due to greater lift. However, the greater drag on the left wing will slow it up so that the glider will yaw to the left — just the opposite of a coorinated turn. Imitate this motion with a ruler and you will see the problem. The solution is to limit the upward deflection of an aileron to a fraction of the downward deflection of the opposite aileron. Thus, the drag forces can be balanced out.

The principle methods of controlling yaw is to add sweep to the wings and a tail surface behind the center of gravity. Sweep in the wings helps prevent yaw by creating a greater angle of attack on the wing that rotates forward and thus greater lift and drag. This wing then rises, slows and swings back to the original position. A vertical tail surface will act very much like a fin on a water ski or surfboard to keep the glider moving straight ahead. A raised keel pocket or rudder will serve this purpose.

This review of roll and yaw control allows us to assemble an overall view of the forces on a glider in a turn. Figure 67 shows the top view of a glider in a constant, co-ordinated (non-slipping) turn. Assume the glider and pilot to weight 200 LBS. and the wing span to be 31 FT. Furthermore, take the angle of bank to be 45° and the airspeed at the keel (center) of the glider to be 20 MPH. This is a realistic consideration for a high performance design. By using the equation for circular motion given in the previous section, we can calculate the radius of the turning circle. This

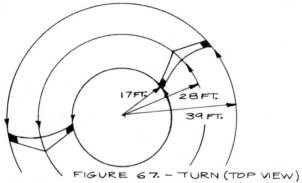

FIGURE 67. — TURN (TOP VIEW)

radius is approximately 28 FT. In a 45° bank the wing span will only be 22 FT. as seen from above. Therefore, the inside tip will have a radius of 17 FT. and the outside tip a radius of 39 FT. Each section of the glider completes the circle in the same amount of time, so that the outside tip must have an airspeed of nearly 28 MPH while the inside tip has an airspeed of 12 MPH. Since the outside tip is traveling at over twice the airspeed of the inside tip, why doesn't the glider lift the outside wing and roll over? The answer is not simple, but lies basically in the fact that the angle of attack varies continuously along the wing. If a constant bank angle is maintained, the entire wing descends at the same rate. However, horizontal speed increases as one moves along the wing towards the outside of the circle (see figure 68). In addition, dihedral, sweep and other roll control factors combine to produce stability in a turn. It is significant to note that a turn produces a continuous yawing action (one wing moves faster than the other) so that sweep tends to make a glider roll out of a turn. A designer can make a glider tend to roll out of any degree of bank turn, or stabilize at a given bank angle all by adjusting the glider's configuration. The pilot learns to coordinate the amount of push-out with the bank angle for a given design. By adjusting push-out, he adjusts the airspeed until both wings are creating equal lift and the glider executes a smooth, non-slipping turn.

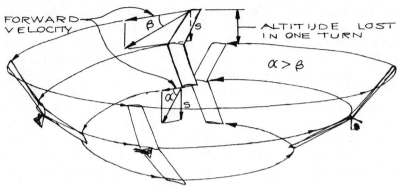

FIGURE 68. - ANGLE OF ATTACK IN A TURN

STALLS

Besides the problem of slipping in a turn, there is the danger of stalls. To understand how to avoid or overcome a stall in a turn, we will look at their cause. As discussed in Chapter II, a stall occurs when the glider's wing is at such a sharp angle to the airflow that smooth flow over the surface is impossible. The air has mass, and therefore, has a resistance to change in direction due to inertia. In figure 69, we see how the shape of the upper surface of the airfoil affects the angle of attack at which the wing stalls. In general, a more cambered (rounded) upper surface will allow the airflow to change more gradually and thus be operable at a higher angle of attack.

FIGURE 69.- CAMBER AND STALL CHARACTERISTICS

A related subject that often crops up in aerodynamics discussions is the Reynolds number. This is simply a way of expressing the ratio of the inertia forces to the viscous forces in a fluid or gas. The Reynolds number for a hang glider is around 1,000,000. In this case, the inertia of the air is the most important factor affecting the stall characteristics as well as the production of lift and drag. A dandelion seed, on the other hand, has a very small Reynold's number and the viscosity of the air is the most important factor determining its flight. The many tiny hairs of the seed actually interfere with the air molecules and float happily along without the use of an airfoil. A hang glider would experience the same thing if the air were as viscous as molasses. It is important to calculate the Reynolds number for a given wing when making scale models. It is found that a model more than one sixth the size of the original wing will have such different stall and flight characteristics that the model's behavior will not be a valid indication of how the full-size wing will operate. It is worthwhile to note that the wing tips of many hang gliders are much smaller than the center (root) section. Thus, different parts of the wing will not stall at the same angle of attack.

In a turn, a glider will experience a heavier wing loading. This can be seen in figure 63 and is due to centrifugal force. A glider will stall at the same angle of attack, regardless of wing loading, but the flight speed will increase. Figure 70 shows the increase in stall speed, wing loading and sink rate as the bank angle increases. Straight ahead flight is represented by zero degree bank. Note that at 60° the stall speed doubles.

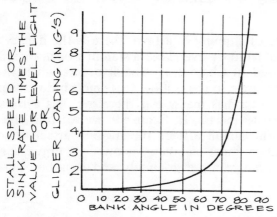

FIGURE 70. — CHANGES IN A TURN

In addition, the wingtip on the inside of a turn is at a high angle of attack and is traveling much slower than other parts of the wing. Consequently, a stall occurs more readily when a glider is in a turn, and the inside wing is the first to stall. This is why a pilot flying very slow must speed up before entering a turn. If the inside wingtip does stall, the lift is reduced, the drag is increased and the glider enters a flat spin. Like a maple seed, the glider turns within its own span and loses altitude rapidly. Since part of the glider is stalled, it will not respond to the normal roll-out control. The pilot must first pull the bar in to pick up speed, get the stalled portion flying, then roll-out. In a weight-shift glider it is not too hard to regain control in a flat spin. (It is more difficult when ailerons are used since the aileron on the inside wing will also be stalled). However, the danger lies in the fact that the glider may turn back into the hill before the pilot has time

68

to recover. In a high wind this could be disasterous. The designer can help alleviate the spin problem by adding wing twist or washout. This is a gradual lowering of the angle of attack toward the tips as shown in figure 71. All hang gliders use this method of preventing tip stalls. A straight ahead stall (the pilot flies level and slows to the stall point) will invariably result in the tip stalling first and a spin unless washout is employed.

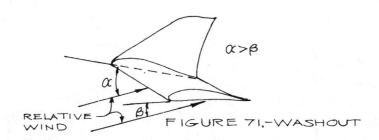

RELATIVE WIND   FIGURE 71.-WASHOUT

Before investigating how washout is achieved, we should clear up the matter of high speed stalls. If a glider is moving at a fast rate, as in a dive or a slip, it is possible, by pushing the control bar out rapidly, to increase the angle of attack to the stall point before the glider has a chance to slow down. This high speed stall results in a very rapid dive. This is obviuosly deadly near the ground. The only good part about a high speed stall is that it relieves structural loading during a rapid pull-out from a maneuver. If a glider will stall before the maximum wing loading is exceeded, then the danger of in-flight breakup is avoided. The same principle applies in turbulence. If the gusts stall the wing before they over-stress it, their effect will be limited to causing control problems.

WASHOUT AND PLANFORM

The early standard Rogallo wings had a washout problem. There was washout at the tips, but also too much at other points along the wing. In figure 72 (a) we see how the portion of the sail between the tip and the center is turned up in the rear or washed out for the standard design. This means that this section is flying at a much lower angle of attack and developes much less lift than it possibly could. One solution would be to tighten the sail, but the small tips would also loose washout and create spin problems. The real improvements came with the use of battens and roach. Battens are stiff rods which are inserted in the sail and allow a portion of the material to extend beyond the limit of the keel and leading edge. This is shown in figure 72 (b). In flight the unsupported outer portion of the sail lifts up and gives a very favorable washout curve as shown in the rear view. Most of the twist is at the tips. Another way of achieving this tip washout is to use a short piece attached to the leading edge at the desired angle. This is the well known "truncated tip" shown in figure 72 (c). Tip washout is usually limited to a few degrees.

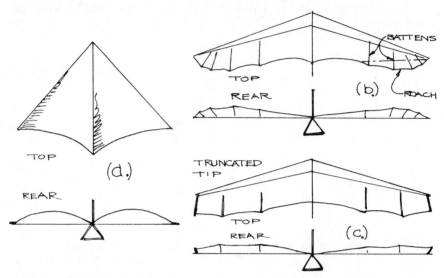

FIGURE 72. - OPTIMIZING WASHOUT

A gratifying property of roach tips is their ability to vary washout at different speeds. At higher speeds when there is no danger of a stall, washout is not needed, and indeed is undesireable. A roach tip is free to change its angle of attack and will do so to minimize drag as the speed increases. A truncated tip is usually not "free-floating" so at high speeds creates excessive drag and thus hurts performance. Truncated tips also imply extra hardware and more weight at the tips.

Truncated and roached tips brought about better glide ratios in two ways. First they allowed the sail to be tightened since the washout now could be controlled. National Aeronautic and Space Administration studies showed that reducing billow is the most effective way of increasing glide ratio. Billow is the amount in degrees that the sail will spread out beyond the airframe. Presently, there are successful designs employing zero degrees of billow.

The second improvement was better lift distribution. Figure 73 shows a standard and a high performance glider with the areas producing the most lift and drag mapped out. Note that the high performance glider has a much wider chord at the tip and thus produces lift all the way out. A rear view of the span-wise loading on a glider at different angles of attack is shown in figure 74. The increased tip loading which, in turn, produces tip washout at high angles of attack is evident.

70

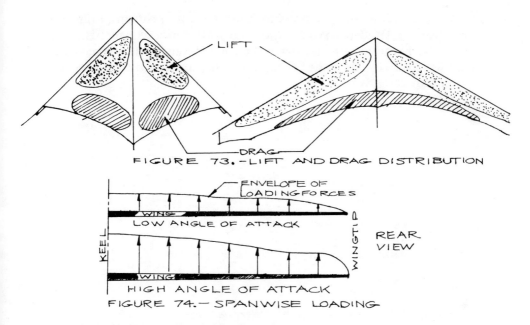

FIGURE 73.—LIFT AND DRAG DISTRIBUTION

FIGURE 74.— SPANWISE LOADING

PERFORMANCE AT SLOW SPEEDS

One of the main considerations of slow speed flight, the stall, has already been discussed. Another important consideration is minimum sink rate. It is desireable to have a glider sink as slowly as possible. Increasing the size of the glider for a given weight pilot (decreasing wing loading) is one way to achieve this. However, this factor is limited by the reduced control associated with lighter wing loadings. Increasing the camber of the airfoil will produce a lower sink rate up to a point. Increasing the billow by a small amount will give a better sink rate at the expense of glide ratio, since the added billow will increase the camber.

One of the most useful ways to better the sink rate as well as the glide ratio is to increase the aspect ratio. To understand this we must look at the cause of losses in performance at slow speeds. At a high angle of attack, the wing is disturbing the air greatly. There is a high pressure area below the wing and a low pressure area on top. The air wants to equalize this pressure and does so by rushing out behind the wing as well as around the tip. This produces a wing tip vortex as shown in figure 75. This phenomena can be observed in twisted vapor trails left by jets. Slowly run your hand through your bath water at a high angle of attack and you will see a vortex or swirl. The flow of the air across the bottom of the wing does not cross it directly, but becomes increasingly span-wise as the wing tip is approached. This indicates a loss of efficiency. Indeed, almost all the lost energy in a glider at slow speeds is due to the creation of wing tip vorticies. Pilots do not fly directly behind another aircraft due to the dangers

71

of encountering these energetic swirls. Vorticies are most pronounced at the slow speeds related to landing and taking-off. Ground effect is caused mainly by the reduction of the vorticies by interference when the glider is close to the ground. The glider flies more efficiently and seems to float on a cushion of air.

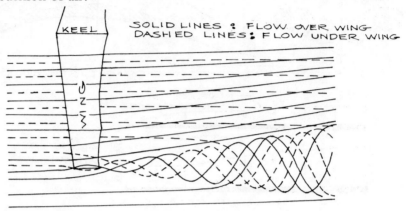

FIGURE 75. — WING TIP VORTEX

Various methods of reducing the loss to wing tip vorticies include tip plates, diffuser tips, vortex gates and increasing aspect ratio. The first three are pictured in figure 76. Note that birds such as seagulls have diffusor tips while birds such as vultures, hawks and eagles reduce tip vortices by spreading their primary feathers and reducing the pressure difference at the tip similar to a vortex gate.

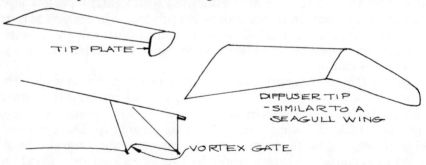

FIGURE 76.— METHODS OF REDUCING VORTICIES

The aspect ratio is the ratio of the span to the chord. A higher aspect ratio means a longer, thinner wing. The two wings in figure 77 have the same area. Note how much more tip chord is present in the low aspect ratio wing. There will be less pressure difference between the top and bottom at the tip and thus, less of a vortex for the high aspect ratio wing. This reduction of energy lost at the tips represents an increase in efficiency which means a better sink rate and glide ratio.
Over the years, the aspect ratio of hang glider designs have risen steadily.

The practical limit to aspect ratio is structural strength and roll control. A long, thin wing of sufficient strength is hard to build without increasing the weight beyond the carrying ability of the pilot. Most hang gliders do not have a uniform chord length throughout their width. Therefore, since

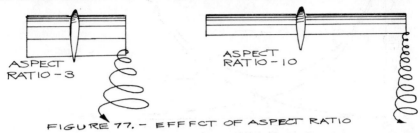

FIGURE 77. — EFFECT OF ASPECT RATIO

the span times the average chord equals the surface area, an expression for aspect ratio is: A. R. = b^2/S, where b is the span and S is the surface area. This formula can be used to find the aspect ratio of any wing. This physical characteristic is one of the most important in determining a glider's performance, and is often quoted in discussions and ads concerning a certain design.

A good glide ratio (L/D) for a given airfoil design depends on two things: maximizing aspect ratio and decreasing parasitic drag. Parasitic drag consists of the drag on structural parts (form drag) and the wing (profile drag). A certain amount of profile drag is necessary to create lift, so reducing form drag deserves much attention. When a solid moves through a fluid, pressure differences in the front and back disrupt the flow and cause turbulence (eddys). The energy in the turbulence comes from the solid and represents a loss in the form of drag. In order to reduce drag it is necessary to reduce the turbulence. One method is to give the solid a smooth surface. Thus, coated cables create about 19% less drag than uncoated cables of the same diameter. Another drag reduction technique is to eliminate sharp corners and curves on the solid through the use of fairings (see figure 78). It is apparent that the prone flying position presents much less resistance to the airflow (less drag) and thus results in a better glide ratio.

TUBING IS STREAMLINED BY THE USE OF A FAIRING. FAIRING SHOULD BE ABOUT 3.5 TIMES WIDER THAN THICK

FIGURE 78.— STREAMLINING

In chapter II it was noted that the total drag (Dt) consists of two parts, parasitic drag (Dp) and induced drag (Di). Induced drag represents the loss of energy related to producing lift. This is essentially contained in the wing tip vorticies. Consequently Di is greatest at higher angles of attack (slower speeds). The parasitic drag increases with the square of the velocity. Thus, the two parts of drag will combine as in figure 79. Note

73

that the angle of attack for best L/D is at the point where Di=Dp. The angle of attack for best sink rate is at the point where Di=3Dp. It should

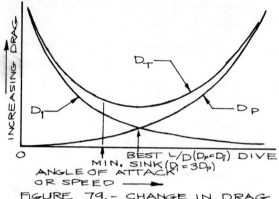

FIGURE 79. – CHANGE IN DRAG

be clear that a designer has to reduce drag by any means possible in order to have a top flying craft. A picture of the total drag on a hang glider is presented in figure 80.

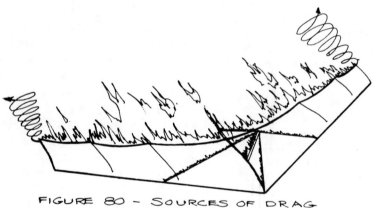

FIGURE 80 – SOURCES OF DRAG

PERFORMANCE AT HIGH SPEEDS

It is useful to have a reasonably high rate of maximum flying speed to penetrate high winds and travel cross-country with good time. Of course, any glider will attain high speeds in a steep dive, but it is necessary to have a good glide ratio at higher speeds. This is mainly determined by airfoil design. A thin airfoil usually has a better glide ratio than a thick airfoil at high speeds.

Methods of increasing the top speed of a glider consist mainly of reducing drag. Less billow will create less drag. Cambering the leading edges also helps since this allows the leading edge to follow the curve of the trailing edge and thus reduce profile drag. Unless other changes are made, increasing the span to increase the aspect ratio will result in a lower maximum speed. This is because of the greater frontal area. A sail that breaks down (flutters) at high speeds will create greater drag than a smooth sail and tend to reduce the top speed. The dangers of high speeds are those mentioned previously — structural damage due to high loads when encountering turbulence or maneuvering.

Another consideration of high speed operation is dive stability. At higher and higher speeds, the glider should develop a strong tendency to slow up, or pull out of the dive. If it does not, it is divergent and will tend to nose down and flip upside down or stabilize in a steep dive. In Chapter II, we found that an airfoil by itself has exactly this tendency. However, a careful use of sweep, reflex, washout control, camber and center of gravity placement can produce a pitch-stable glider. Figure 81 shows the planform of a glider and the quarter chord sweep. It is found that the resultant force on an airfoil will move according to angle of attack. At a high angle of attack this will be as far forward as ¼ the chord length back from the leading edge. This point can be considered the center of pressure,

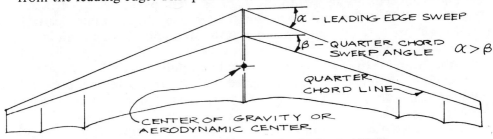

FIGURE 81 — QUARTER CHORD SWEEP

or more correctly, the aerodynamic center. If the upward forces along the wing are considered to be located on the ¼ chord line, the designer can calculate where to place the center of gravity. At higher speeds, the tips of a variable washout glider produce less lift so that the center part of the wing is the main portion flying. If the center of gravity is behind the location of the center of pressure, the glider will tend to nose up. If the center of gravity is not behind the center of pressure, reflex can be added to move the center of pressure forward. Truncated tip gliders with fixed washout can operate safely without reflex in the keel, while battened roach tip gliders usually require reflex for pitch stability. A lower center of gravity will have a helpful effect on pitch stability since the drag on the sail at higher speeds will operate through a longer moment arm to pull the nose up. Camber in the keel has an adverse effect on pitch stability due to the divergent properties of a cambered airfoil.

Pitch response is also determined by many factors. Quick response means the glider reacts immediately to the pilot's back and forth control bar movements. This means there is little pitch damping. A certain amount of damping is necessary so that the pilot will not overcontrol and cause the glider to oscillate wildly. Sweepback in the wings is a principle source of damping in pitch. A non-swept, thin wing will vary pitch much easier than a wing swept as much as a standard Rogallo.

75

SUMMARY

In this chapter we have looked at some of the important physical principles in hang glider flight. An analysis of the strength of a glider was made and the main cause of structural failure was found to be maneuvering and encountering turbulence at high speeds. The important thing to remember is to slow down in gusty conditons. Hopefully, all gliders will be designed to stall and relieve their stresses before they break apart.

Turns were found to be a complex chain of events and combination of forces. Obviously, the pilot doesn't have to think about these details when he flies, but he can learn more about how to optimize his turns by analyzing his control actions in relation to glider reaction. A good turn is a continuous, constant movement. Any turn will loose more alitiude than straight forward flight, due to the apparent increased wing loading. A well coordinated turn will minimize this alititude loss.

The main dangers in a turn are high speed slips and stalls. The stall speed in a turn is increased according to the bank angle. A pilot learns to feel his glider in a turn and fly close to the stall point without initiating a spin. A well designed glider will use washout to help prevent spins. The variable washout tip was a great boon to hang gliding in that it allowed the washout to optimize at different speeds. Although the birds use variable washout, the designers of hang gliders were truely pioneers in this development.

Slow speed flight and methods of improving performance was investigated. Two principle means were found to be increasing the aspect ratio and decreasing drag. Drag is made up of induced drag and parasitic drag. To reduce induced drag we must work with tip design and eliminate wing tip vorticies. To reduce parasitic drag we must streamline our bodies and glider structures. This will also improve the top speed capabilities of the glider.

The ultimate goal of any designer is to maximize all flight capabilities while minimizing complication, set up time and weight. Unfortunately, in reality a constant trade-off must be made between each design criteria. Weight is the factor which limits performance in hang gliding. There are many gliders with incredible performance, but these are not pilot portable. Progress is being made, however, with new materials and techniques appearing to constantly extend our horizons.

CHAPTER VII

ADVANCED FLIGHT

One problem with learning to hang glide is you return to earth too soon. The experience is so thrilling that you're sorry it has to end. The solution is learning to soar. Soaring entails seeking out rising air currents and riding them for hours. Sound like fun? There's nothing that excites a hang glider pilot more than a soaring wind with a few thermals attached.

To learn to soar you must polish your skills to safely handle a variety of flight conditions. Once again the best approach is a process of increasing your skills gradually. The pilot that works on the basics will be a better flyer in the long run. Making a mistake can give you a scare that prevents progress for months. Take things slow and have a good time.

ADVANCED TAKE-OFFS

By now you have perfected your take-offs under normal conditions. You should be accomplishing them automatically. A good take-off is a smooth movement that progresses from the run to leaning into the glider to flight. Once you master the technique, there is no conscious control movement as the act of lying down (for prone) sets the control bar at the right position. Learn to do calm wind take-offs. This requires a vigorous run. Get the glider lifting its weight with a few strides then run as fast as you can. The whole secret is keeping the proper nose angle throughout the run. A downwind launch can be made if you can run fast enough. Try this only after you can easily launch in no wind and then never attempt launching in more than a light wisp of downward air.

A very common occurance is for the wind to blow up the hill during the day then start flowing down as evening approaches. This is due to the heating and cooling differential between the lower and higher areas of ground surface. Often you may climb or drive to the top of a hill at the end of a perfect day only to find the wind has started to drift down hill. You may be able to do a good downwind take-off, but by the time you get set up the down current has increased. You can bet that it will continue to increase. This is where your judgement comes in . Many accidents have occured from just this situaton. There is a limit to how fast you can run to prevent a nose-in.

A crosswind take-off is possible but also has its limits. These limits are the strength and the angle of the wind. To reduce the effect of a crosswind, you can run across the hill (into the wind), dip the upwind wing slightly or turn the glider into the wind and run down the hill. Don't try taking off in a wind angling more than 45° to the hill, and then, only if it's just a breeze.

In general, you should find a steeper hill easier to take-off from since it's easier to get flying speed. Remember, every foot you drop is equivalent to moving forward a number of feet equal to your glide ratio. This is the problem with a cliff launch. In calm conditions you must run fast enough to prevent a stall when you step over the edge. The biggest problem an inexperienced pilot faces on cliff launches in a calm is getting the nose too high and stalling at the edge. To prevent this, practice running on a flat area until you can keep the glider level and really get some speed in a short distance. All the running practice you did as a beginner pays off here. It is best to try your first cliff launch at a site with a slight slope leading to the edge. Many areas have ramps that are suitable for learning. It is better to have the nose a little too low than too high. Indeed, If the runway is short, you must run with all you've got then dive a bit off the edge to gain flying speed. It's not as fearful as it sounds and can be very much fun. Watch other experienced pilots many times before you try, and solicit their advise.

A windy cliff launch is an entirely different matter. If the wind is over 10 MPH (16 KPH) you must have assistance (an experienced cliff launcher can launch alone in higher winds). The reason for this is twofold: First, there are rotors and turbulence associated with cliffs (see figure 82). A rotor is a swirl of air that stays about in the same place. Turbulence is random, erratic swirls of air. These effects are caused by the sudden change in direction of the ground at the cliff edge. The air simply can't make such a

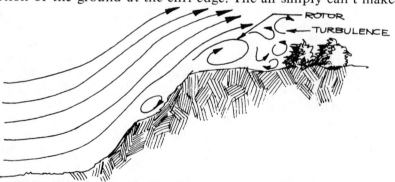

FIGURE 82.— ROTORS AND TURBULENCE

sharp turn. On a smaller scale, rotors and turbulence can be seen behind a truck in a snowstorm. Learn to visualize them by watching the path of grass or leaves thrown into the wind. The other problem is the wall of uprushing air at the edge of the cliff that catches the glider's nose first and thrusts it upward. This invariably throws the glider out of control and

78

back over the take-off area. Pilots call this a blow-back. Even in a light wind with a running take-off you must be ready to hold the nose down as you go off the edge.

To do a proper windy cliff take-off you must get as much of the glider out into the smooth flow of the air as you can. This means having a friend on the nose wires as close to the edge as he can get. He should always have a safety rope tied to his waist. Without this rope he will be reluctant to get you as close to the edge as you should be. The nose wire man should hold your cables firm until you get in position and ready to fly. He then angles the nose downward until he feels no pressure up or down (see figure 83). On your command he lets go and ducks quickly as you step off the edge and into the sky.

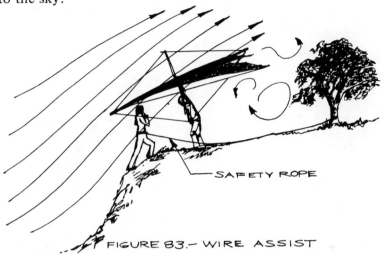

SAFETY ROPE

FIGURE 83.— WIRE ASSIST

When there is strong turbulence or a rotor present you may need two additional helpers on the side cables. They should always let go first and stand ready to grab the cable if a gust lifts the wing. Use an experienced pilot for a nose man for the first few times. He will tell you what to do and help you set the proper nose angle. When you tell him to release, don't hesitate — fly.

The holding position that gives you the most control and best run is that pictured in figure 46(a). The reason this isn't recommended for beginners is that it can lead to arm injuries if a nose-in occurs. Learn to use it on a gentle hill. After a few take-offs it will feel natural.

THE 360

A complete circular turn is a necessary maneuver for thermal soaring. More than any other aspect of hang gliding, the 360° turn has been cast as a villan. It has injured pilots. This is unfortunate, since it is not that hard a maneuver to do. The problem lies in perception. In reality a 360 is the same as any turn only held for a longer period of time. Figure 84 (a) shows the top and side view of a 360 in zero wind. The glider describes a neat circular path. In 84 (b) assume that a 10 MPH wind is blowing into the hill. In this case the pilot starts the turn at exactly the same place, but the downwind portion of the turn (labeled X) is elongated due to the wind. On the side view we see the pilot almost hit the hill. If the wind had been blowing stronger he would have had a serious accident. The way to prevent this is do the 360 faster (this means more entry speed, more bank and more push out) to spend less time drifting towards the hill. Another way to keep it safe is to wait until there is much more clearance from the hill to start the turn. It should be apparent that at certain wind velocities at a given site there is no way to do a safe 360.

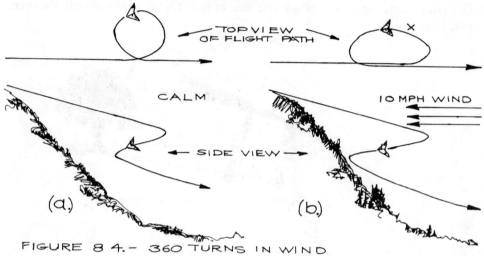

FIGURE 84.— 360 TURNS IN WIND

Another judgement problem occurs when turning into the downwind portion of the turn. Here the glider accelerates due to the tailwind and the pilot misjudges ground speed for airspeed and pushes out to slow down. This causes the deadly downwind stall. Flying downwind into a hill is gambling with hopeless odds. You must learn to recognize the changes that occur when turning away from the wind and into the wind. The truth of the matter is there is **no** difference in control in a downwind or upwind turn (except close to the ground – see Chapter V). The difference is in perception. Don't let anyone tell you otherwise. The situation is similar to a boat in a fast river. If you can't see the bank you don't know which way you are turning in relation to the water.

Learn to train your senses gradually. Do your first 360 in no wind over a large landing area with at least 500 FT. (150 M) altitude. The reason you need this much height is that initial tries at 360s invariably end in diving (slipping) turns that loose incredible altitude. The pilot simply didn't push out enough. Avoid this problem by doing a wide, gently banked 360 at first. Concentrate on airspeed and control. Do many of them, working in both directions with steeper banks and smaller circles. You should do countless 360s in calm conditions before trying them in any significant wind.

Avoid doing 360s in heavy turbulence. The gusts can stall you in any portion of the turn or tip you into a sideslip. Another thing to avoid is looking up at your outside wing. This is one of the quickest causes of vertigo. Vertigo is a disorientation caused by the body sensing forces that don't relate to what the eye is seeing. It is not pleasant to be suspended in the air and not know which way is up. If vertigo occurs center yourself on the bar and focus on something close by (your nose cable) until things settle down. You build up your tolerance to vertigo as you gain experience, so simply don't overdo things. Only do multiple 360s by adding one or two at a time. There's no rush — teach yourself in careful steps.

EXPERIENCING LIFT

By now you may have felt lift on take-off or during some portion of your flight. What causes this? The answer is simply an upward movement of air. There are three causes of organized upward air movement. We shall deal with each of them in turn. First, we must investigate the requirements for sustaining flight. If we recall that every glider has a minimum sinking velocity we can immediately see that if the air has an upward component of velocity equal to the glider's sink rate then altitude will be maintained. The secret is to find the areas where the air has this upward movement (lift). For hang gliders these areas are near ridges, in thermals, in waves or convergence zones. All of this lift is a result of energy exchange in the lower atmosphere. This means moving air and possible turbulence.

At times in a soaring flight great altitudes are achieved and unfamiliar landing areas are used. Learn to tell wind direction from various signs. Watch for smoke and ripples on water. Watch the trees to see which side is fluttering in the breeze. Always be on the lookout for power lines. If the field is near a house you can bet there are wires. Look for poles — the lines are hard to see.

By the time you attempt to soar you should be relaxing in flight. The extended periods in the air can tire you rapidly if you are tense. The lift may be glassy smooth or rough as ocean chop. In turbulence you may have to hang on firmly, but can still relax most of your body. The technique of hooking your feet on the rear cables (when prone) has a stablizing effect and greatly reduces your struggles. Flying supine is also relaxing. A supine harness lets you lean back in easy living fasion when combined with a foot stirrup (see figure 28). When you learn to relax you can enjoy the view and your surroundings, which is the real fun.

RIDGE SOARING

Ridge soaring is the most basic form of extending flight. Many pilots master the necessary skills with less than a years experience flying hang gliders. To ridge soar you must be able to perform efficient, smooth turns and fly near minimum sink speed in higher winds.

To understand the principles of ridge soaring look at figure 85. Here is a side view of a ridge or hill with the wind coming directly in. When the wind hits the hill it is deflected upwards, and thus, produces the lift needed to sustain the glider. If we let the arrows X, Y and Z denote the wind speed and direction of different points we can see that only Y has a significant upward component. Only inside the dashed line is the lift great enough to soar. This area is called the soarable envelope or lift band.

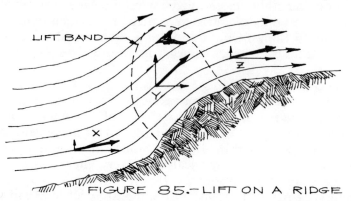

FIGURE 85.—LIFT ON A RIDGE

A pilot that wants to stay in the lift band must fly parallel to the ridge as in figure 86. To do this he must crab to the left and right. If he flies straight out from the ridge he will soon be out of the lift band. If he directs his nose parallel to the ridge he will be blown over the top. The crab angle is directed more perpendicular to the ridge as the wind velocity increases.

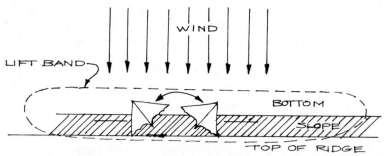

FIGURE 86. — RIDGE SOARING

The amount of lift available depends on the following: (1) The angle of the slope — the steeper the better. (2) The height of the slope — the higher the better. (3) The width of the face — the wider the better. A ridge is much better than a hill since the air can go around the hill instead of over it. (4) The strength of the wind — the stronger the wind the better, up to the point of danger. (5) The angle the wind hits the hill — a perpendicular wind is best. The lift drops quickly as the wind begins to cross.

You can learn to soar on a day with smooth 15 MPH (24 KPH) winds. As soon as you take off and clear the hill, turn to direct your flight path parallel to the ridge. Follow this heading until you come to the end of the ridge or you have risen above the crest. Now do a smooth shallow turn back the other way. In one day of practice you can be soaring successfully.

Here's what to look out for:

1. Turning too late on take-off. Most beginners wait too long to turn and thus fly out of the lift. One note of caution: always turn in the direction of the wind on take-off if it is crossing. The reason for this is there is a wind gradient close to the slope which can roll you into the hill.

2. Turning too often. If the lift is very light it will take time to rise to maximum height. A turn always loses more altitude than minimum sink flight. In marginal lift conditions, make your passes long with few turns.

3. Flying too far away from the ridge. When you first learn to soar you may be fearful of getting too close and thus not fly in the best lift. Flying too close to the ridge is of course dangerous. The best lift is over the steepest part of the slope.

4. Flying too fast. Your best sink rate is at a speed just above a stall. In very light lift you must fly this speed constantly. Do not stall however. At best you will lose plenty of altitude recovering. At worse you will be blown back into the hill.

5. Gaps and breaks in the ridge. These are outlets for the wind so there is a lot of air rushing through them. Be ready for this and angle away from the ridge to cross them. Often you will notice no difference when crossing a gap, but be prepared for stronger winds.

Landing on top of the ridge is a very satisfying feat. You avoid having to regain the top for another flight. Only do this after you've had plenty of soaring and landing experience. When you have lots of altitude turn tail and fly back over the ridge. Do a 180 and land into the wind. Watch out for rotors and turbulence. If the hill is rounded the landing should be smooth and uneventful. You can land fairly close to the edge. If the hill is steep with a sharp edge you may have to land well back to avoid turbulence. This is an advanced maneuver — don't try it without watching an expert pilot first.

The following "rules of the ridge" should be memorized to prevent mid-air collisions (see figure 87). (1) When approaching another glider, pass to the right (a). (2) When overtaking another glider, pass between him and the ridge (b). (3) Make all reversing turns away from the ridge (c). (4) When entering a thermal circle in the direction established by gliders already in the thermal (d).

THERMAL SOARING

Using thermal lift is a bit more difficult than using ridge lift. To see why, we must investigate the nature of a thermal. Look at a pan of boiling water. See the bubbles forming? They adhere to the bottom while they grow, then break off to rise briskly to the top. The exact same process occurs in nature. The sun heats up certain surfaces quicker than others and produces bubbles of hot air which grow, then break off and rise. A pilot can learn to detect this rising air and circle in it while he climbs higher. Watch a hawk's lazy circular flight. If you see him gradually going up then he has "hooked a thermal".

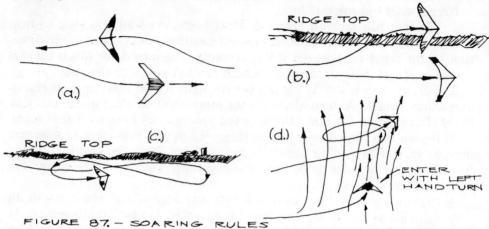

FIGURE 87. — SOARING RULES

The surface areas that produce thermals best are parking lots, ploughed fields, dried grass areas or bare rocks. These areas are heated much more readily than vegetation which tends to dissapate the heat. The size of the thermal is determinéd in part by the size of the area producing it. Higher winds will tend to break the thermal away before it grows large.

An ideal thermal appears as in the drawing in figure 88. Note that the greatest velocity is in the center or core of the thermal. There is an area of downdraft around the thermal and possible turbulence. When a wind is presented the thermal may not be so nicely formed, but leans with the wind and becomes eroded. A thermal will rise until the air cools to the point that any moisture it contains is condensed and a cloud forms. This is the familiar cauliflower or cotton puff cloud. Thermals can exist without producing clouds if the air is dry. These are called "blue thermals".

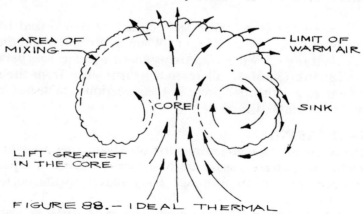

FIGURE 88. — IDEAL THERMAL

You have probably already flown into thermals and experienced their bumps and lift. The technique is to circle in the middle of the thermal.

84

Since we cannot see a thermal this isn't easy. One solution is to use instruments. These are altimeters and variometers. An altimeter is a device which tells you how high you are. It works on the principle that pressure drops with altitude. A variometer tells you if you are going up or down and at what rate. When you are in strong thermals you can feel the initial upward acceleration, but if you continue steadily upward the senses can no longer detect the upward movement. This is where a variometer becomes a handy tool. In light, "scratchy" thermals a "vario" is indespensible for maximizing lift.

If you can't afford a variometer (a realistic situation since they cost well over $100), try using all your senses to find the lift. Often when passing into a thermal the air will feel warmer or even carry scents from below with it. The thermal drifts with the wind, so learn to watch your ground track and vary it accordingly. The first indicator of a thermal will be a bump of varying severity. If you are off to one side of the thermal one wing may be lifted. If the thermals are light you can quickly turn towards the lifted wing and find the center. If the thermals are "booming", it may feel like a sky hook is holding your wing up. The only thing to do in this case is complete a 270° turn started by the roll and catch the thermal head on (see figure 89).

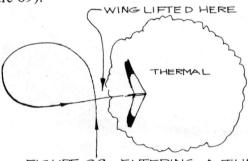

FIGURE 89.- ENTERING A THERMAL

Once you enter the thermal, you circle to stay within the lift and ride as high as you can go. This may be from several hundred to tens of thousands of feet. Part of the fun of flying thermals is going from one to the other cross-country. This isn't as easy as it sounds. First, there is usually areas of sink between the thermals and lots of distance. It is typical for thermals to be spaced about four times their maximum height. This means a 4/1 glide ratio is required just to get from one to the other in conditions with no sink. The best method is to spiral up, fly downwind fast until the next thermal is found then slow down and spiral up again (see figure 90). On any given day the thermals can be of many different sizes and strengths. A good pilot will be flying back and forth like a shark looking for a meal.

Hang glider pilots almost always combine thermal soaring with ridge soaring. This is because they need the ridge lift to stay aloft until they find a thermal. A ridge or hill is a thermal collector. The reason for this is a thermal will drift with the wind. A light thermal may be rising only a few feet per minute while a strong thermal can produce several thousand

FIGURE 90. - CROSS COUNTRY IN THERMALS

feet per minute lift. The top of the thermal rises about half the actual upward velocity of the center (see figure 88). Thus, the thermal will often have a great sideways drift and be blown into the ridge (see figure 91). Once it hits the ridge it is deflected upward. In this manner, a large number of thermals from various distances away from the ridge will be concentrated along the slope. On a good thermal day you can often ridge soar even though the actual wind is low.

PATHS OF THERMALS

FIGURE 91. - A RIDGE AS A THERMAL COLLECTOR

One of the potential hazards of thermal soaring is associated with the fact that if you catch a thermal on a ridge you must turn 360s close to the top and eventually fly over the back to follow the thermal downwind. If the wind is very strong you must expect downdrafts, rotors and turbulence on the backside of a ridge. Airplane pilots consider 1000 FT. (300 M) to be a safe altitude to fly over a ridge.

Another thermal hazard is the possible existance of strong turbulence. When flying in turbulence, remember to slow down to a good maneuvering speed. Flying too fast increases the gust loading and the chances of structural failure. At altitude you may stall, but the glider will still be intact. A real problem exists on landing in exceptionally strong thermal days. A thermal breaking off can throw you around out of control when you are close to the ground. Land a little faster in these conditions to maintain quick response.

Flying into a cloud is foolish for two reasons. You become disoriented when you lose contact with the ground. Tests have shown that you can be in a turn and not know it. Cumulus clouds resulting from thermals tend to have glider destroying turbulence in them, especially when associated with towering thunderstorsm. Pull out of a thermal before the harmless looking white monsters engulph you. Some pilots have found themselves sucked into the cloud by a powerful thermal. Keep an eye on your vario. If it indicates more than 1000 feet per minute up, head for the edge of the cloud and be ready to run for it. There is a small possibility of experiencing lift outside the cloud. A thermal entering greater winds at higher altitudes will be moving slower than this wind and will act like a ridge to deflect the air. It is a difficult feat to reach this in a hang glider.

Thermal soaring is certainly a challenge. It combines all the skills a pilot learns in normal flight with the need for imagination, calculation and just plain luck. Again the key to learning the art is practice. Eventually you'll be flying along and your harness straps will strain as you shoot upward. Hold on — you've hooked a big one!

WAVE SOARING

Waves occur in the atmosphere just like they do on the water. In the air, waves are usually caused by surface irregularities such as mountains, ridges, hills or even buildings. Under certain conditions, when the wind is deflected upwards it rebounds back down then back up in a continuous process like a weight on a spring. We can see in figure 92 how the waves continue downwind from the ridge producing them. Note that along with the lift in each wave is a sink area of equal intensity. The waves form in rows parallel to the ridge so that soaring in them requires flying parallel to the ridge. When the air is on the upswing the moisture may condense and form lenticular clouds. When these clouds don't exist it may be hard to tell where the wave is. It is predicted that waves exist about 75% of the time (mostly at night). It is no wonder that pilots experience mysterious areas of lift unrelated to thermals.

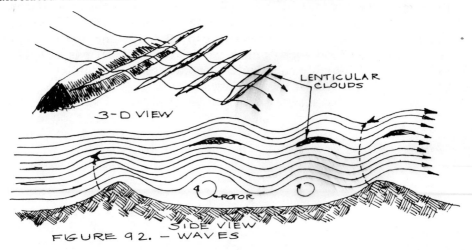

FIGURE 92. — WAVES

You cannot enter a wave from the mountain that forms it. You can, however, catch a crest from an elevated site spaced suitably downwind. The best sites for wave soaring are those with smooth ridges upwind from take-off. The problem with this, and the danger of waves in general is rotors and turbulence that occur downwind from solid objects. If the lenticular clouds are ragged, stay on the ground— this indicates strong turbulence. The best wave soaring available is those caused by lower hills on a mild day. The lift in these waves can be as smooth as glass. Large scale waves can hit you like a fly swatter.

A wave can form behind a single rounded hill. Often however, this lift is produced by convergence. This is caused by the flow separated by the hill coming together and producing an upswelling. You can see this behind a protruding rock in a stream.

Another form of lift produced by convergence is when two airmasses or flows of air come together. They meet and the warmer air is forced upward. This can occur when a cool seabreeze meets the warm land mass, or evening downward flow from facing ridges meet in the middle of a valley.

It should be clear that there are many sources of lift for a pilot to utilize. As long as the air is moving or the sun is shining you should be on the lookout for ways to get carried higher. The mark of a expert pilot is his ability to eke out the last bit of lift available in the sky.

SUMMARY

With these aquired skills you should be able to complete both Hang III and Hang IV requirements. The Hang IV tasks requiring figure eights are intended to test your ridge soaring ability. The best place to do this task is on a ridge in soaring conditions. There are special skill sign-offs included in the hang rating program. By now you should be able to pass the cross-country, cliff launch, 360, altitude and turbulence tasks. At certain sites, in certain conditions you will be asked to present proof that you passed these tasks. This is for your own safety, so work on them with an Observer.

When you work towards a goal in this manner, real progress can be noted. The ultimate goal, of course, it to take-off some morning and not come down till sunset over a hundred miles away. This trip is entirely feasible and would certainly be a sightseeing adventure.

CHAPTER VIII

UPGRADING YOUR EQUIPMENT

Every pilot wants to fly higher and further. It's a common thing to expect a new glider to bring this about. This may be true, but just as important is the need to have the equipment you are flying at any one time be in top shape. This chapter explores the best path to take when changing to a higher performance glider as well as how to keep it performing well.

THE HIGH PERFORMER

To select a new "super kite" you'll need to assess the situation in the same manner as outlined in Chapter III. This time you must pay a little more attention to cost of the glider as well as weight. High performance gliders are priced as high as they fly. The weight of this class of glider depends on the designer's choice of structure. Don't comprimise on structural safety to save a few pounds. In the air you won't notice it. Another factor to consider is the wide span of the glider. It may be that your take-off and landing areas just won't accomodate these bigger birds. A landing area that was ample for an intermediate glider may seem to shrink suddenly when your glide ratio increases dramatically.

Most pilots like to choose their colors to please their palate, but a well known aphorism is "white kites fly better". It's a fact that the white sail material is less porous and lasts longer. This is because the resin is not replaced by dye as it is with other colors. The lighter the colors you choose, the better, expecially out at the tips where the stress is greatest.

The difficulty you experience in learning to fly your new glider will depend on your present ability and the design. Certain gliders are much easier to fly than others. Start out on a gentle training hill. The take-off should be easy, but once you're in the sky you may start yawing or Dutch rolling. This latter action is a combination of yawing and rolling. These perturbations are usually pilot induced. You are simply overcontrolling. To correct this, speed up a little and sit still. Before long you'll learn the right amount of imput to use and be flying straight as an arrow.

The biggest problem is landing. A high performance glider is apt to nose in if you don't use precise landing controls. You must learn to approach the ground with the right height and speed then push the nose up suddenly. Often the best way to land a glider when flying prone is to sit up and put your hands on the uprights. This gives you the greater flare needed to stop suddenly and prevent a nose-in (see figure 93).

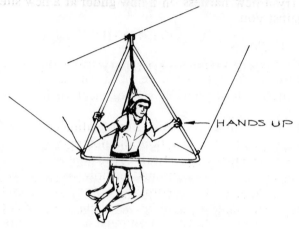

FIGURE 93 .— STAND UP LANDING POSITION

THE HARNESS

The full body harness was mentioned in Chapter III (see figure 27). The added comfort during long flights is well worth the expense. Sometimes these harnesses are cumbersome on take-off. Once again you must learn to use them gradually. Some of these harnesses come with a stirrup and some use knee hangers. If you use a stirrup you need some method of keeping it out of the way while you run. You can glue a piece of Velcro to it which sticks to a piece on the harness or make a tab to hold in your teeth as in figure 94. The stirrup should always have a metal foot rest as shown. Do not attempt to get in your stirrup until you are away from the hill and the glider is under control. Accidents have happened because the pilot was paying more attention to his foot rest than his flying. Stirrups are a bit more comfortable but more confining than knee hangers.

FIGURE 94.— STIRRUP

The supine harness is a good way for a seated pilot to get comfortable and reduce his drag. A foot stirrup as shown in figure 28 is a must. To really lay back you may have to hold on to the rear cables for control. Some pilots rig up hand grips for this purpose.

A good way to find the equipment suitable for you is to trade with a friend. You can learn a lot about different designs in a short time. Treat each new item with respect. Take things one at a time and start on a training hill. Never try a new harness on a new glider at a new site — you have three strikes against you.

REPAIRING EQUIPMENT

Once in a while you may make a slight error: A downwind landing, a bad take-off, a tree landing, etc. You're faced with an expensive repair bill. Many pilots from the do-it-yourself school elect to fix their own. Fine, but do it right!

Tubing repairs are the most frequent. Bent leading edges are common. If the tube is not bent beyond a few tube diameters, you can straighten it. Step outside and hold the tube vertical. This is the only way to see where the bend is since the tube will sag no matter how you hold it. You can use a tire and a friend, as shown in figure 95 (a), or let one end rest on the ground and have your friend hold above the bend 95 (b). The sharper the bend, the closer he should hold to it. You must apply pressure to the bend. The closer your hands are together, the more localized will be the force you apply, Keep them close together for a sharp bend. Carefully inspect the straightened tube for metal fatigue. Ths is evidenced by a white crystalized or pale area on the tube surface. Disgard the tube in this case. When metal is bent it work hardens and becomes more brittle. Therefore, it may be impossible to completely remove the bend as it becomes less flexible. This results in the slight S curve which is frequently observed in a straightened control bar.

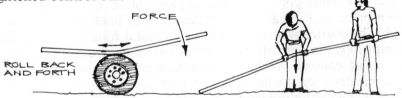

FORCE

ROLL BACK AND FORTH

FIGURE 95. – STRAIGHTENING TUBING

If the leading edge is broken you will have to splice it or construct a new one. If the spar is broken just behind the cross bar sleeve (the most common place) you will have to remove this sleeve and make a longer one. Be sure to have at least three tubing diameters of any tube end covered by sleeving (see figure 26). Use a pop rivet or panhead screw to keep the pieces together. For sleeving, use tubing that is 1/8 inch larger than the inner tube. Be sure to use .058 wall thickness on the sleeve for a snug fit. If you are repairing a glider without deflexors, beware of changing the amount of flexibility of the leading edge. A keel can be repaired in the same manner as a leading edge, but a crossbar should never be straightened or spliced. This member takes a high compression load in flight and must not be weakened. The hints in Chapter III under BUILDING YOUR OWN should prove helpful.

Frayed cables must be replaced. Cut the Nico presses off with a chisel. Place the Nico on a hard surface and use the chisel as in figure 96. Tap it gently then use pliers to pry it apart. You can remove Nicos without damaging the cables if you are altering lengths.

Sail repairs are the hardest to do. If a gormmet is torn out you can sew in a reinforcement patch and replace the grommet. If the sail has a small tear you can tape it. Signal tape (available from sailboat suppliers) seems to work best. Tape the tear on both sides. A larger hole can be patched. Use a hot knife to sear the frayed ends then lay the patch over and sew. Do this on a flat surface and use tape to hold the patch in place. Double sided tape between the patch and the sail works best. If you can't match material, then cut out an interesting design such as a bird or whatever suits your fancy. A quick, yet safe, method of patching is to use contact cement. This works well but shows through on light colors. Use it only on the darker shades.

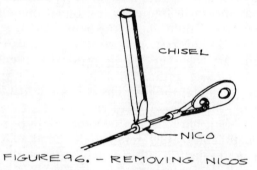

FIGURE 96. – REMOVING NICOS

TRIMMING THE GLIDER

An "in trim" glider will fly hands off between minimum sink and best L/D speeds. Trim can be adjusted by a combination of changing reflex, sail position, sail tightness, center of gravity position or deflexor cable length. Only the last three should be altered by the non-professional.

Common problems are as follows:

1. The glider flies too fast or dives. This means there is too much weight forward or the deflexors are too tight. Try loosening the deflexors first. Most deflexors have turnbuckles you can unscrew. Be sure they are secured with wire safety's when flying. Other designs have a method of changing the length of the deflexors themselves. If loosening the deflexors causes wrinkles to appear retighten them and move your C. G. back by changing your attatchment point. This can be done on some gliders by using an adjustable control bar bracket. A "C. G. adjuster" can be added if more movement is needed (see figure 97).

2. The glider flies too slow or stalls. In this case, the weight is too far back or the deflexors are too loose. Be cautious of tightening deflexors too much. This can make it pitch unstable. Always try one turn at a time. Only adjust the deflexor that points the most vertical if more than one is

92

used. A deflexor angling at 45° will also tighten the sail in the rear portion. If a turn or two on the deflexors doesn't affect the trim noticeably then move the C. G. forward using the methods mentioned above.

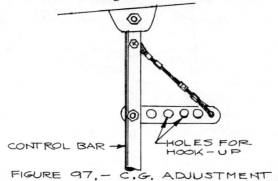

CONTROL BAR →

HOLES FOR HOOK – UP

FIGURE 97. – C.G. ADJUSTMENT

3. The glider drifts or breaks to one side. A common occurance is for a glider to turn one way at cruising speed and fall off on a wing in the other direction upon landing. This is because one deflexor is tighter than the other. In flight the wing with the tighter deflexor generates more lift and tends to roll up. On landing this wing stalls first because the sail is tighter and has less washout. This phenomena usually occurs with misadjusted 45° angle deflexors. To correct this, loosen the deflexor on the lifting wing. When the glider straightens out readjust both deflexors for proper hands off speed. If the problem is severe, you may have a misadjusted sail.

To adjust the sail, check for leading edge tension first. Grasp the sail at the leading edge with the fingers of both hands about an inch apart. Try to pass them around each other. The distance they move is proportional to the sail tension (see figure 98). Make sure both sides are the same. Another important check is for equal billow. Hold the nose of the glider and bring it down until you see the trailing edge of one side just clear the

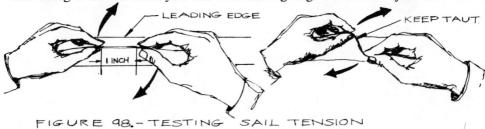

LEADING EDGE

KEEP TAUT

1 INCH

FIGURE 98. – TESTING SAIL TENSION

cross bar. The other side should be in exactly the same position (see figure 99). You can check for both sail and deflexor adjustment very accurately this way. Tightening the sail on one side will make that side stall sooner. You can trade off sink rate and docile handling for glide ratio by playing with these adjustments. Be careful.

The tension of the sail at the keel should be much greater than at the leading edges. This is due to the greater amount of material and seams. The entire sail needs to be stretched the same. If the glider feels "squir-

93

rely" and you don't know what's wrong, take it to an expert or have the factory get it in shape. There are many factors controlling glider stability and trim.

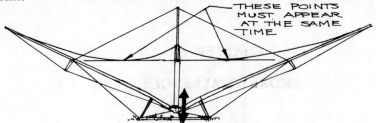

THESE POINTS MUST APPEAR AT THE SAME TIME

FIGURE 99.— CHECKING SAIL TENSION

SUMMARY

Getting new equipment is always fun. The problem is what to buy. You will be inundated by manufacturers claims and dealers promotion. Remember, you're in hang gliding to have fun. Get a glider that is enjoyable to fly. Some designs are great performers but are beasts to fly. You don't need the hassle. Try to fly as many gliders as you can before you buy. You'll be surprised at how different they are. When you do get your new equipment start out like a beginner. You can, of course, be flying high much sooner, but you must re-learn take-offs, in-flight controls, judgement of glide path and landing technique. Take it easy and explore the endless sky.

94

A very satisfying aspect of this unique sport is the fact that it is thrilling at all levels. The beginner has plenty of fun flying from small training hills. The expert doesn't get bored due to the wide variety of flying situations he encounters. In this chapter we look at the many aspects of hang gliding you can explore. Some of these are for experts only, some are for all pilots. The fun comes from learning new experiences and sharing them with friends.

EXPERT MANEUVERS

When a pilot is a few thousand feet over the landing area and the air is smooth he feels like dancing through the sky in graceful swooping arcs. The wind hurtles by and he feels more alive than ever before. He performs spins, multiple 360s and wingovers. He knows his limits and leaves plenty of margin for error.

If you want to share in this fun you must learn these maneuvers very carefully. Try learning them only after you have plenty of experience on your glider and are controlling with automatic reactions. Start by doing tight 360° turns. To do these you must have perfected the coorination of medium banked 360s. Enter the turn with more speed, then roll quickly to the side while pushing forward. You will do a very steep and fast turn. Get the whole maneuver smooth so that you can do multiple 360s with-out varying the angle. The whole secret to steepness on your turn is the speed which you enter it. Learn these gradually. You will feel strong G forces according to how steep the turn is (see figure 70).

There are two forms of the maneuvers called wingovers by hang glider pilots. The first form is illustrated in figure 100 (a). Here the pilot dives for speed then pushes out to climb quickly. Before the glider reaches the stall point the pilot moves to one side of the bar and turns the glider into a dive. As soon as he picks up sufficient speed, the pilot levels out or proceeds into another wingover. In 100 (b) the pilot dives then rolls at the same time he is pushing forward. This banks the glider at a very steep angle, and a very fast 180° turn is made. With sufficient entry speed bank angles in excess of 90° can be achieved. The best way to learn to do wingovers is to start with lazy-8s. These are simply diving and climbing figure

8's (100 (c).

The biggest danger of these maneuvers is the excessive loads placed on the glider and stalling while near vertical. Deaths have occured from both factors. If you wish to try this type of stunting, limit yourself to mild conditions and conservative wingovers. Performing these maneuvers in turbulence is foolish. A small gust can stall you in a radical position. Don't do them for a crowd. Pilots tend to press their limits when in front of the public. NEVER attempt wingovers in anything less than a high performance glider. Don't do any maneuvers at the end of a long flight - your concentration is lowered.

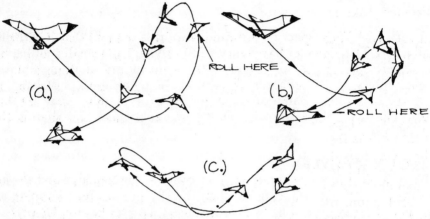

FIGURE 100.- WINGOVERS

Loops have been accomplished on hang gliders. Unfortunately, it's a bit like jumping cars on a motorcycle. There is little margin for error. Until a glider is built specifically for this stunt we respectfully request that you do your crowd pleasing on a motorcycle.

Spins are caused by a stalled wing. The glider will rotate around that wing in a very flat turn. This can be induced on some gliders simply by pushing out too far in a turn. To get out of a spin do not move to the outside of the bar. You must pull in and roll into the direction of the spin to get the stalled wing flying again. Spins are a problem near the ground since the recovery takes a bit of altitude. Try spins with at least 1000 FT (300 M) ground clearance.

COMPETITION

Competition is a phase of hang gliding pilots of all levels of ability can participate in. Beginners can fly distance tasks, time aloft tasks and spot landings. Advanced pilots can fly pylon courses, aerial ballet, speed runs or cross country tasks. The serious competitor must spend time practicing the different events if he hopes to do well.

Spot landings require landing on a specified target. This takes judgment of altitude and velocity as well as the effect of the wind. You can only learn this by spending time hitting spots in varying conditions. The most important factor is setting up a good approach. One method is to imagine a ridge downwind from the spot. You traverse back and forth at this point until you reach the right altitude to turn toward the spot. Once you are committed to a direct line towards the target, you can adjust for altitude by flying at different speeds, or standing up to increase your drag. Another technique consists of losing excess altitude upwind of the target, then making the classical downwind, base and final approach (see figure 59). Whichever method you use, you must learn to land on your feet at a standstill. You lose points if you touch the ground with anything but your feet.

Distance tasks require you to fly as far over the ground as possible. Turns around pylons may be part of the tasks. In zero wind velocity, you simply fly your best L/D speed. If you are flying into a headwind, you must fly faster than your best L/D speed. In a tail wind you must fly slower than this speed. How much faster and slower depends on your glider's performance and the strength of the wind. Try flying different speeds in wind to detect the differences. If the course includes upwind and downwind legs, you must vary your speed as you change direction. If a portion of the flight is through areas of lift slow down to take advantage of the extra height you'll gain. Obviously, airspeed indicators and variometers are useful here.

If you are flying a pylon task that requires the first part of the flight to be at a minimum time and the second part at a maximum, a higher wing loading is advantageous. You should fly the first portion of the task faster than your best L/D speed and the second portion at your minimum sink speed. The closer the target is to the take-off, the faster you fly at first. If you are in a course where you must perform figure 8s around two pylons, always go between the pylons on a downwind leg (see figure 101). This minimizes the amount of turn necessary due to the crab angle. In light wind enter the course in the direction that gives the shortest flight path.

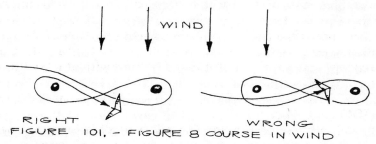

FIGURE 101. – FIGURE 8 COURSE IN WIND

When rounding pylons in general, it is best to come in wide then cut close on exit (see figure 102). This sets you up well for the next pylon and is more efficient.

One of the most important aspects of a competition flight is the take-off. If you are competing for speed, distance or time aloft the energy acquired by a powerful run can be turned into extra height or distance. A poor take-off can break concentration and affect the entire flight.

FIGURE 102. — ROUNDING PYLONS

CROSS COUNTRY

Flying cross-country is the goal of many pilots, whether for the purpose of achieving awards, setting records or simply watching the scenery. The United States Hang Gliding Association has set up requirements for pilots to earn pins called Otto Lilillienthal awards after the great aviation pioneer. To achieve these awards you must fly for a certain time, cover a certain distance and reach a certain height. There is a provision for both a one way flight and a goal and return flight. The latter consists of reaching a distant point then returning to the take-off area.

To learn to fly cross-country a pilot has to master soaring techniques. If he follows a ridge line the pilot must learn to shoot gaps and maximize his speed. On strong days the best way to make good time down a ridge is to move away from the slope so that you enter lower winds. This lets you point your nose down the ridge and make better time. When thermaling, you make the best time by flying fast between the thermals, then rising as quickly as you can. Fly downwind to get the best one-way distance.

A large part of the success of a good cross-country pilot is his preparation. To have a chance at a distance flight you should learn to watch the weather. Cold fronts bring thermals in northern areas. Find out ahead of time when the winds are going to be favorable. Learn everything you can about micrometeorology (small-scale air movement) and meteorology. A friendly weather station or airport weather service can be a great help.

Know your terrain. Part of preparation for a cross-country venture is to look at topographic maps to find where the best lift will be. Drive along looking for gaps, power lines, steep parts of the slope, thermal generators and every other part of the landscape likely to help or hinder your journey

If you are planning to try for any type of record you must obtain a barograph and various forms to make it official. A barograph is an instrument that records the altitude of your flight. Write the USHGA to get a complete information sheet on the procedures to follow. If you plan a long flight into hostile country, it is wise to carry water and a small survival kit. Many pilots attempting to "go-for-it" have landed in peculiar places. With the proper preparation your normal Sunday flying can be turned into an exciting sky trek.

TANDEM FLYING

After a great flight every pilot wants to share the experience with a friend. One way to do this is take the friend along. Tandem flying opens up a whole new area of communication. The finest thing is to be soaring free with your lover by your side. You share the controls and point out the sites to each other. Of course, you must take ample safety precautions. Never start from a high site. An inexperienced person may "freeze up" and pull in on the control bar. Even with experienced pilots there may be trouble in running. Learn to run together on the flat then work your way up the training slope. One person should be in command at all times. Work this out before hand.

It is best to fly seated when trying tandem flights unless you have a very wide control bar (see figure 103). Two people inside the control bar doesn't leave much room for movement. If you do fly prone, make sure each harness has a separate suspension rope. Adjust these so both flyers are hanging at the same level in flight. With a seated harness, either tie two individual seats together or use a single seat wide enough for two.

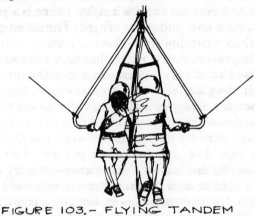

FIGURE 103.- FLYING TANDEM

Be aware that your take-off, stall, landing and normal flying speed will be greatly increased by the extra wing loading. It would take much longer to recover from a stall - beware. The controls will feel sluggish due to the higher forces involved. Expect to run a bit on landing. Don't try to take-off in zero wind. Approach tandem flying sensibly and it can be the most fun you've ever had.

Flying with more than one glider together is called "relative work". This is great flying especially when you do maneuvers together or fly close enough to talk. Be careful not to fly too close behind another glider. The vortices can toss you around radically (see figure 80). If you ever touch wingtips one glider should dive and the other slow up. This will prevent the hardware from hooking. There is no excuse for flying this close, however. Keep plenty of clearance from another glider in turbulence. Midair collisions are dangerous.

FIXED WINGS

There are many pilots who take their first flights on fixed wings. However, they are generally harder to learn on than flexible wings. The term

99

"fixed wing" refers to a general class of hang gliders whose main characteristic is that they have rigid wings and do not fold up like a Rogallo. Of course, there are a wide variety of designs.

The advantages of fixed wing hang gliders is their potential for better performance. This is because the rigid structure of the airfoil can keep the optimum shape all the way out to the tips. Also, they can be more easily combined with aerodynamic controls which saves energy on long flights.

The disadvantages of fixed wings is their cost, weight, complexity, storage problems and set up requirements. For different individuals in different situations, some or all of these problems may be overcome by the advantages. Fixed wings certainly add to the interest of the sport and have the greatest potential for far reaching cross-country flights.

When learning to fly a fixed wing, follow the steps outlined in Chapter IV. This means caution and gradual progression. The controls may be a bit more difficult and the consequences of nosing in more drastic. It is helpful to have a light wind when flying fixed wings as they often have a faster take-off speed. Extend your abilities slowly, even the slightest accident can result in a costly repair. Some of the designs require an assistant on the tail during take-off. Be sure to train him thoroughly. Newer designs are directed toward doing away with this extra hand. The sport is certainly continuing to produce better and better designs. Fixed wings are a major part of this advancement.

TOWING

If you live in the flatlands you're probably tired of all this talk of mountains, ridges and hills. You know there are other ways to get aloft. One of the most popular is towing. This is done most commonly behind a boat over water. Like all facets of hang gliding, towing has changed dramatically over the years and continues to do so.

At the present, regular hang gliders with reinforced or special control bars are being safely towed. Wing loadings have gone up resulting in lower towing speeds. Safety equipment and techniques have been added. In years past, two of the biggest problems were break-up of gliders and accidents resulting from towrope breakage. The first problem has been reduced by using stronger gliders with deflexors and a two point tow system called a bridle (see figure 104), limiting the angle of climb. The problem of rope breakage is relieved due to the increased stability of the gliders and the pilot's ability to react with a wingover if a sudden radical pitch up occurs.

The real solution to both problems is including a weak link in the tow rope. What this does is prevent excessive force to build up. The rope will break before enough energy can be stored in the glider to pitch it up to a radical angle. The Federal Aviation Administration (FAA) regulates the towing of gliders under section 91.17 and 91.18 of the General Operating and Flight Rules. These rules dictate that a portion of the tow rope have a breaking strength of between 80% and 200% of the maximum operating weight of the glider.

The third problem related to towing is the possibility of "lock out". Have you ever watched a child's kite oscillate at the end of the line then nose dive into the ground? This is a lock-out. Lock-outs occur most often when following a boat in a turn or flying in a cross wind. To prevent them the pilot must remain over the wake of the boat in a turn and keep the upwind wing low when flying down wind of the boat in a crosswind. If a lock-out occurs, the boat must be slowed immediately to provide slack in the tow rope. The pilot can then fly the glider back behind the boat. It is apparent that the handling of the boat is crucial when towing. The only safe arrangement is to have a driver and a throttle man. The throttle man is facing backwards and controlling the boat speed. He also has a line to an emergency release on the tow rope. The driver and throttle man should be well versed in how to handle different problems. They are ultimately in control of the flight.

For equipment you need a suitable glider with a special control bar. High performance gliders are not the best tow gliders due to their yaw tendencies. A mid-range glider is recommended. The control bar must be specially built or reinforced to handle the extra stresses involved. A release mechanism must be included on the bar. Floats on the glider and a floatation vest for the pilot are essential (see figure 104).

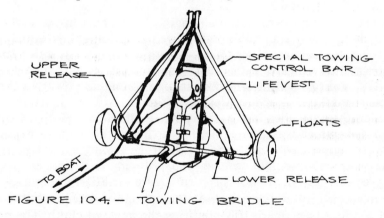

FIGURE 104. — TOWING BRIDLE

The boat should be capable of traveling 40 MPH (64 KPH) if downwind towing is planned. An engine size of 75 HP is recommended. Any length rope can be used, but most tow ropes are between 500 and 1000 FT (150-300 M). This rope should be free of frays, cuts or knots.

Towing over land can be accomplished by auto, winch or snowmobile. The problem with land towing is that the driver can't readily see what is happening to the pilot and yet must control the throttle. A trained observer sitting next to the driver is absolutely necessary. He should be able to release the tow rope in an emergency. Sailplane tow releases work well for this purpose.

You should only learn to tow under the guidance of an instructor or expert tow pilot. The ideal situation is to be already proficient at flying before you try towing. Then, all you need to learn is how to take-off and climb to the top of the line. The take-off with the least potential for mistakes is performed on water skis. Flying speed is achieved gradually. The beach start is the best way for a good flyer. Here the line is paid out and the boat travels into the wind at 18 MPH (29 KPH) less the wind speed. When the line tightens the pilot pops off about 10 FT (3 M) then climbs slowly to 100 FT (30 M) to minimize danger. After this he can climb quickly to the top of the line.

Beware of shear layers. These are movements of air with different velocities at different altitudes. If you tow into significantly faster moving air you will suddenly increase the force on the glider. Keep the angle of attack as low as possible to prevent this undue loading. Once you are as high as you can get, pull in to slacken the rope, then release. You will be flying free as any bird.

ENGINES

Another form of hang gliding without a hill that is gaining popularity is motor gliding. In this case an engine is fitted to the glider to provide energy for climbing flight. After reaching an altitude of several thousand feet the pilot stops the engine then hunts for lift. A good pilot can stay up all day on one tank of gas.

For the successful operation of an engine – glider set-up, several criteria must be met. First, the minimum power requirement is equal to the weight times the minimum sink rate. A simple calculation shows that this isn't too hard to achieve with the engine since it is less than two horsepower. The real problem lies in converting the engine power to thrust in an efficient manner. Propeller design is the crux of the matter. To fit a hang glider the propeller has to be quite small. However, this requires a higher R.P.M. which is undesireable. If the tips travel too fast they lose effectiveness due to cavitation. This is the formation of a vacuum and a shock wave, greatly increasing drag and reducing lift. Longer propellers help solve this problem, but in turn create location problems. Some engines have been mounted near the king posts, and some further back on the keel.

Most engines weigh around 35 LBS (15 KG). Placing this weight too far back from the center of the glider makes the whole affair hard to balance on take-off. Short keel gliders are the best choice for this reason along with their favorable performance characteristics. This amount of mass placed behind the pilot has dangerous implications in the event of a crash. The spinning propeller is a lethal devise if it breaks loose. It is necessary to have a switch held in the mouth to keep the engine running. Spit it out and the engine stops, thus eliminating the propeller threat.

A major concern when adding an engine to a glider is placement so that the thrust doesn't radically change the trim of the glider. If the thrust line is too high the glider will dive. If too low it will stall. Of course the weight itself changes the center of gravity. This must be compensated for by the thrust and pilot movement.

It is interesting to note the effect of flying at different speeds. Flying at your minimum sink speed will give you the best rate of climb. Flying at best L/D speed provides the most efficient climb in terms of fuel consumption. Remember, changing the throttle setting changes the angle of climb, not the speed of the craft. To change the speed you must change the angle of attack.

When learning to fly with engines always start by perfecting your take-off and landing from a small slope with the engine turned off. Then try the same thing with the engine at low R.P.M.s. Eventually work up to full power take-offs. Remember the increase in speeds that will accompany the extra weight. Also be sure to wear cotton in your ears. The engines are LOUD.

When you put an engine on your glider you are legally termed an airplane and consequently must be licensed by the FAA. The process involves getting your glider inspected for airworthyness, filling out forms and taking one lesson of dual instruction in a conventional aircraft. You will then receive an experimental rating. This amount of work is insignificant when you consider the potential for hours of flying free from the necessity of a good high launch point.

BALLOON DROPS

Balloon drops have been popular for years. It's not hard to understand why. Imagine being carried aloft to around 10,000 FT cutting loose and floating for the next hour. The altitude of drop is limited only by the experience of the balloonist.

To do a balloon drop you must first obtain clearance from the FAA. Again there is an inspection to pass and forms to fill out. The paperwork mainly involves the balloonist since he is the one regulated by the FAA. Your hook-up between the glider and the balloon must be approved. The easiest way to assure approval is to use standard aircraft materials when constructing the system. You must have a release for the pilot and one for the balloonist. Sailplane releases work best here.

Most drops will have to be in the early morning or evening since the balloon must go up in minimal wind. Some pilots use a rope to the nose to keep from rotating, but this is not necessary and adds complications. Work your plans out specifically with your balloonist. You should pre-arrange your drop altitude. Before you release,the balloon should be descending several hundred feet per minute. This will prevent him from shooting upward and bursting his envelope when your weight is cut loose. You should expect to dive suddenly when you pull the release. It is best to have a method of pulling the release with both hands on the bar for good dive recovery. A balloon drop should never be attempted by an inexperienced pilot. There are plenty of pilots around who have dropped from a balloon — solicit their guidance.

THE FUTURE

Trying to predict the future of hang gliding is like betting on the horses. You must gamble on past performance. With this in mind we can safely predict that the sport will continue to grow in popularity just as the designers continue to come up with impressive improvements. The performance of the gliders has increased in leaps and bounds. The progress shows no signs of letting up. There will be a limit however. This is because all design changes that lead to better performance ultimately end up adding weight. There is, of course, a weight limit to foot launched gliders. Some eminent changes like the removal of crossbars and cables in favor of other configurations appear to lighten the glider. This is true to a certain extent, but when these designs reach their full potential the weight will be increased.

The coming years will provide many interesting fixed wing designs. These ships will be an amazing improvement over the current offerings. Glide ratios will be 20 to 1. At this point, true cross-country flying will be realized. The builders and pilots working with these designs at the present are true pioneers, on the level with many past great men of aviation.

As we enter more and more into the realm of the flight capabilities of conventional aircraft, we face the spector of FAA involvement. To remain self-regulating there is only one requirement. We must maintain the safety of hang gliding and learn the rules of flying applicable to all aircraft. As long as we have the training to prevent encounters with airplanes, the FAA doesn't want to spoil our fun. We can maintain this balance by supporting the self-regulating organizations in the sport. It is up to each individual pilot to participate in the Hang Rating Program and help preserve our freedom. In this manner we will gain our well deserved reputation as the greatest pastime ever invented.

APPENDIX I
HANG RATING PROGRAM

The following is a summary of the USHGA hang rating program: You must complete the tasks listed and have an instructor or observer witness and sign them off in your log book.

HANG I
1. Set up and preflight glider
2. Un-assisted take-off
3. Safe, straight flight controlling airspeed and making minor corrections
4. Pass an oral exam.

HANG II
1. Land three times in a row within a prescribed circle whose radius is determined by 10 x L/D max. of the glider.
2. Complete linked 90° turns. These turns must alternate from left to right (or vice versa) and demonstrate smooth control.
3. Pass an oral exam.

HANG III
1. Hold a Hang II rating for at least two months with 30 flying days and at least 90 flights.
2. Demonstrate steep and gentle 180° linked turns along a pre-determined track.
3. Land three times in a row within a circle whose radius is determined by 5 x L/D max. of glider.
4. Complete at least 10 flights with 75 FT. (or greater) ground clearance.
5. Demonstrate speed control in turns and various wind conditions.
6. Pass a written exam.

HANG IV
1. Hold a Hang III rating for at least four months during which he will have made at least 60 one-minute flights. Five flights each must be made at five different Hang III sties (at least three inland).
2. Make 5 five-minute flights.
3. Soar above take-off for at least 5 minutes on three different flights.
4. Complete 5 flights with at least 250 feet ground clearance.
5. Demonstrate figure eights around preselected pylons across the wind. Course must be flown smoothly with equal radius turns.
6. Land three times in a row within 20 FT of a spot after flights of at least one minute.
7. Approach downwind within 75 FT of a spot. Make a 180° turn within 100 FT past the spot and land within 50 FT of the spot.
8. Pass a written exam.

SPECIAL SKILLS
At present there are seven additional skills that a Hang III or IV pilot can get signed off. These are required at certain sites.

1. Turbulence
Demonstrate controlled flight in conditions requiring quick, deliberate, correct and substantial control application.

2. High Altitude
Accomplish flights in which terrain clearance exceeds 1000 FT for at least three minutes. In these flights, 720° turns must be demonstrated (in both directions). The pilot must have flown over 10 minutes. All flights must be foot launched.

3. Cliff Launches
The cliff must be precipitous and over 100 FT high. Launches must be either un-assisted in near calm conditions, or assisted in windy conditions.

4. Cross Country
Pilot must recognize and safely land in an area not visible from take-off. He must be able to explain ways to determine wind direction and the presence of obstructions from aloft. Must be able to explain effects of wind, lift or sink on glide path.

5. 360° Turns
Pilots must perform 360° in both directions, entering the turn slow and ending the turn fast, and vice versa. Rollout from the turn must be smooth with no slipping evident.

6. Towing
Pilot must demonstrate his ability to launch safely with a standing land start, or a sliding beach start. Must demonstrate the ability to track behind the tow vehicle through a turn and pass an oral test concerning towing signals and emergency procedures.

7. Auxiliary Power
Pilot must demonstrate safe take-off procedures including minimum distance take-off and take-off followed by a landing within 5 seconds. Must demonstrate steady climb and flight at various power settings. Must demonstrate slow flight including two 180° turns with at least 20° bank. Must pass an oral test relating to power trim changes.

HANG V
This rating is reserved for pilots with total knowledge, maturity and experience in the sport. To be eligible, a pilot must pass an Instructor Certification course, hold a Hang IV rating (with all the special skills) for 3 years and get the signature of three Observers attesting to his safe flying.

APPENDIX II

LILLIENTHAL AWARDS

This USHGA program is set up to award achievement as a pilot progresses. An application from a USHGA observer should be filled out for
each award. The requirements for all awards are:

1. The pilot must be alone in the hang glider.
2. A flight may count for only one leg of an award.
3. Pilot must use a pilot carryable hang glider. Launch must be on
   foot (skiis are permitted).
4. A USHGA Official Observer must witness the entire flight or a
   Barogram may be submitted. An Official Observer is a USHGA
   Examiner, Observer, Instructor or any member who has earned a
   Hang Rating or a leg of a Hang Award. A barogram is a tracing
   from a barograph mounted on the glider.

BRONZE AWARD

A. A flight lasting one minute is required.

SILVER AWARD

A. A flight lasting one hour is required.

B. A flight over 6.2 M (10 KM) is required.

GOLD AWARD

A. A flight over 31.1 M (50 KM) is required.

B. An out-and-return flight around a point at least 6.2 M (10 KM)
   away is required. Landing must be within a radius of 1.25 M
   (2 KM) of launch point.

GLOSSARY

AILERON — A control surface on a wing tip which changes the lift and drag and thus raises the wing.

AERODYNAMICS — The study of the movement of a body through the air. This is applied to hang glider wings.

AERODYNAMIC CONTROLS — Moveable surfaces used to control the glider. These consist of elevators, aerilons, dragelons, elevons and rudders.

A-FRAME — Control bar.

AIRFOIL — A curved surface designed to generate lift when moving through the air.

AIRSPEED — The velocity of the glider through the air.

AIRSPEED INDICATOR — An instrument for measuring airspeed.

ALTIMETER — An instrument for measuring altitude above a predetermined point.

ATTITUDE — The amount of nose up or nose down. Pitch.

ANGLE OF ATTACK — The angle the relative wind makes with the chord of an airfoil.

AN PART — Any piece of hardware certified for use in aircraft.

ASPECT RATIO — Ratio of the span to the chord or span^2 divided by surface area.

BANK ANGLE — The angle the wings make with the horizontal in a roll.

BATTENS — Stiff shafts inserted in the sail to hold shape.

BILLOW — The slack in the sail when placed on the glider frame (measured in degrees by spreading the sail).

BLUE THERMALS — Thermals that don't produce clouds due to low moisture content.

BUSHINGS — Small metal tube inserted in a hole drilled in a tube for added strength.

CABLE — Twisted strands of steel wire used for bracing.

CAMBER — The amount of curvature on the upper surface of an airfoil.

CARABINER — An oval ring used to attach the harness to the glider.

CENTER OF GRAVITY — The point along the keel where the pilot's weight is suspended.

CENTER OF PRESSURE — The point along the keel where the resultant of the lift and drag is considered to be acting.

CHORD — Measurement of a wing from the leading edge to the trailing edge.

CONTROL BAR — A triangular set of three tubes used for support and steering.

CONTROL BAR BRACKET — A bracket held by the heart bolt used to hold the control bar to the glider.

CROSS BAR — A spar running perpendicular to the keel and holding the leading edges in place.

DAMPING — Tendency of a glider to resist motion in a particular direction. Damping in pitch is the tendency to stay at any given angle of attack.

DEFLEXOR — A metal support holding a cable (deflexor wire) to prevent bending in a leading edge.

DIHEDRAL — An upward angling of the wings from side to side.

DIVERGENCE — Tendency for a glider to enter a steeper dive when flying fast.

DOWN TUBE — One of the uprights on a control bar.

DRAG — The energy losses on the glider due to the friction and mass of the air.

D-RING — A carabiner.

GAP — A break in a ridge or mountain chain.

GLIDE ANGLE — The angle between the glide path and the horizontal.

GLIDING — Flight that continues from an elevated point to a lower point.

GLIDE PATH — The flight path of a glider.

GLIDER — An aircraft that remains flying through the energy of gravity only.

GLIDE RATIO — The ratio of the distance traveled forward to the distance dropped. This is used interchangeably with L/D.

GOAL AND RETURN — A cross-country flight to a point and back.

GROUND EFFECT — The apparent cushioning of air beneath the glider close to the ground.

GROUND SPEED — The velocity of a glider over the ground. This is different from airspeed if any wind is present.

GROSS WEIGHT — Total weight of the glider and the heaviest weight possible.

HARNESS — A suspension system that supports a pilot and attaches him to a glider.

HEART BOLT — The bolt holding the king post and control bar brackets to the keel.

HORIZONTAL BAR — The lower tube on a control bar.

KEEL — The spar running down the center of a glider.

KINGPOST — The upright bar on top of the glider used to support the wing when not in flight.

KING POST BRACKET — The bracket holding the bottom of the kingpost to the keel.

KNEE HANGERS — Straps with support lines used to hold the legs up while flying prone.

LEADING EDGE — The forwardmost part of a wing. The spar that forms this forward part.

LIEBECK AIRFOIL — A high camber airfoil used on particular hang glider designs.

LIFT — Uprising air used by the pilot to soar.

LIFT TO DRAG RATIO (L/D) — A comparison of the lift forces to the drag forces. See glide ratio.

LOCK-OUT — An out-of-control swinging of the glider to one side with a subsequent nose dive while towing.

LOOP — A maneuver when the glider starts with a large amount of speed then noses up and continues over the top.

LUFFING — Flapping of the sail at high speeds.

MANEUVER — Flying any path other than straight and level. Examples are turns and wingovers.

MAXIMUM GLIDE RATIO — The best possible glide ratio for a given pilot and glider combination.

MINIMUM SINK RATE — The slowest descent rate possible with a given pilot and glider combination.

NICO PRESS — Nickle-copper fittings squeezed on cables to hold them firmly.

NOSE ANGLE — The angle between the leading edges. Typically 82 to 120 degrees.

NOSE — Apex or forward point of the glider.

NOSE-IN — An accident where the pilot lets the nose get too low on take-off or landing so that the wind forces the nose to the ground.

NOSE PLATE — The plate holding the leading edges and keel together at the nose.

PIP PIN — A pin used for quick fastening in the place of a bolt.

PITCH — Amount of nose up or nose down. Movement about a lateral axis. Altitude.

QUICK RELEASE — A strap for attatching a harness to a glider with a pull line for quick detatchment.

RADIAL TIP — A design feature incorporating battens in a fan shape at the wing tips.

REFLEX — An upward bending of the tail of the keel to prevent dives.

RELATIVE WIND — The apparent wind as the glider is flying. Since the glider is always falling in respect to the air around it the relative wind is different from the actual wind.

ROACH — The addition of sail beyond the imaginary line connecting the end of the keel and leading edge. Roach is held in place with battens.

ROLL — Lifting or dropping a wing.

ROOT — The center of the wing. The keel on Rogallos.

SAFETY PIN — An AN pin used to keep nuts from turning off bolts.

SINK — Falling air which makes the glider travel downward faster than normal.

SKID — Sliding toward the outside of a turn.

SLEEVE — A short tube used to hold a splice together. A sleeve can be on the inside or outside of the tubes.

SLIP — A falling to the inside of a turn due to insufficient push out.

SOARING — Flight extended beyond the normal glide path of the glider.

SPIRAL INSTABILITY — Tendency for a glider to roll with no control movement from the pilot.

STABILITY — Tending for a glider to return to level flight from any attitude or roll.

STALL — A sudden loss of lift due to an excessive angle of attack.

SUSPENSION LINES — Rope used to connect the carabiner to the control bar or the main support straps of the harness itself.

SWAGE — A Nico Press filling.

SWEEP — The angling back of the leading edges.

TANG — A flat piece of metal with holes for connecting cables to bolts.

TELL-TALE — A piece of yarn or cloth on the glider to tell wind direction at take-off.

THIMBLE — A metal fitting used to protect the inside of a cable loop when fastening cables to tangs.

TOW LINE — The line used to tow gliders with a vehicle.

TRAILING EDGE — The rearward part of a wing.

TRUNCATED TIP — A wing design incorporating a short spar parallel to the keel at the wing tip.

TURBULENCE — Gusts or swirls of air encountered in flight.

TURKEY LINE — A line tied to the top of the kingpost for an instructor to use to prevent nose-ins.

TURNBUCKLE — A threaded devise for shortening cables.

VELOCITY — A measurement of the speed and direction of motion.

VERTICAL DIVE — A dive with the nose pointed straight at the ground.

VORTEX (TIP VORTICES) — The swirling of air at the tips of a glider.

WASHOUT — A twist in the wings yielding a gradual lowering of the angle of attack from the keel to the tip.

WIND GRADIENT — Slowing of the wind as the ground is approached.

WIND SOCK — A cloth tube mounted on a pole to indicate wind direction.

WING BOLT — The bolts holding the leading edge to the end of the cross bar.

WING NUT — A nut with metal tabs which can be tightened by hand.

WINGOVER — A maneuver in which the glider follows a path like that of a bike riding up and back down a curved wall.